Unconditional Love

MARRIAGE EDITION

**GIVE AND RECEIVE UNCONDITIONAL LOVE
AND MAKE YOUR MARRIAGE LAST FOREVER**

Also by Dr. Dwayne L. Buckingham

Unconditional Love, Marriage Edition (Workbook)

You Deserve More, A Single Woman's Guide to Marriage:
How to Select and Invest in a Lifetime Partner

Resilient Thinking: The Power of Embracing Realistic and
Optimistic Thoughts about Life, Love and Relationships

The Empathic Leader: An Effective Management Model for
Enhancing Morale and Increasing Workplace Productivity

Qualified, yet Single: Why Good Men Remain Single

Can Black Women Achieve Marital Satisfaction: How
Childhood Nurturing Experiences Impact Marital Happiness

Unconditional Love: What Every Woman and Man Desires
in a Relationship

A Black Woman's Worth: My Queen and Backbone

A Black Man's Worth: Conqueror and Head of Household

www.realhorizonsdlb.com

Unconditional Love

MARRIAGE EDITION

**GIVE AND RECEIVE UNCONDITIONAL LOVE
AND MAKE YOUR MARRIAGE LAST FOREVER**

Dr. Dwayne L. Buckingham, LCSW, BCD

An Imprint of RHCS Publishing

Unconditional Love, Marriage Edition

Unless otherwise indicated, all scripture quotations are taken from the King James Version of the Bible.

To protect the confidentially and privacy of individuals who have shared their stories, identifiable information has been modified.

Additional copies of this book can be purchased on-line at www.realhorizonsdlb.com or by contacting:

R.E.A.L. Horizons Consulting Service, LLC
P.O. Box 2665
Silver Spring, MD 20915
240-242-4087 Voice mail

Expanding Horizons by keeping it "R.E.A.L."

FIRST EDITION
Cover designed by Visual Arts
Library of Congress Control Number: 2015938016
ISBN: 978-0-9855765-7-8
Edited by Lauren Westy and Sharon Taylor

For Worldwide Distribution
Printed in the United States of America

Dedication

To every married woman and man who desires to give and receive unconditional love.

Message to Married Women

Nurture your mind just as much as you nurture your heart. Do not allow your heart to do what your mind cannot handle. Learn to think, feel and do. Feeling and doing without thinking is a recipe for disaster. Love without regret. Do not hold grudges. Experience unconditional love and change your life. Equip yourself with proper knowledge about how to love your husband unconditionally, not with resentment or anger.

Message to Married Men

Loves starts in the heart, not in the mind. You get what you give. Do not allow your mind to do what your heart cannot handle. Thinking and doing without feeling is a recipe for disaster. Love whole-heartedly without straddling the fence and experience unconditional love that will change your life. Expressing unconditional love for your spouse enables her to do the same for you. Equip yourself with proper knowledge about how to love your wife unconditionally, not apprehensively or fearfully.

My hope is to empower you to love unconditionally as you build and sustain a heartfelt marriage.

I wrote the poem on the next page to inspire you. I hope that you enjoy your journey as you explore what it means to *Love Unconditionally*.

Love Unconditionally

I will give you my heart and not fight or flee,

But only if you love me unconditionally.

Love me for who I am, not who you want me to be,

And I will always love you unconditionally.

Don't take my love for granted for it's yours to keep,

But only if you love me unconditionally.

I will love you with all my heart and not resist what is to be,

But only if you love me unconditionally.

I am not perfect and have character flaws, as you may see,

But love me for who I am, not who you want me to be.

I have experienced pain and despair as you can see,

But will give you my all, if you just love me unconditionally.

To earn my love, this is the way it has to be,

And I apologize that I can't give love like God,

which is Unconditionally!

Acknowledgments

I would like to acknowledge and thank all of the married couples that I have worked with over the past 17 years. My ability to understand and teach what it means to love unconditionally would not be possible without your willingness to share your thoughts and hearts. Thanks for fighting for love and striving to give and receive unconditional love.

Contents

THE ONLY LOVE THAT ENDURES IN MARRIAGE

Why settle for love when you deserve to be loved unconditionally? Marriage can be challenging at times, but mainly because we lower our expectations and struggle to live up to our vows. Over the past seventeen years I have spent thousands of hours as a psychotherapist helping hundreds of married couples restore happiness and love in their marriage. Some couples seek therapy in an attempt to save marriages that are ending, while others seek therapy in an attempt to enhance marriages that are good, but could be better. Poor communication, disrespect and mistrust are commonly presented as contributors to marital discord. However, after sorting through the presented issues, we often discover that the lack of *unconditional love* is the underlying problem. Failure to receive unconditional love is one of the primary causes of most failed or troubled marriages.

The desire to be loved unconditionally is the underlying motive causing most men and women to say "I do" at the altar. We enter marriage with the belief that unconditional love is possible and achievable. In the beginning, we are filled with excitement and a willingness to do whatever it takes to make our marriage work. However, if we are denied unconditional love early in our marriage, some of us move forward with apprehension and uneasiness. We may give and receive love at some level, but with a guarded heart.

The desire to be loved unconditionally is the underlying motive causing most women and men to say "I do" at the altar.

In the pursuit of unconditional love, some spouses exploit their partner either emotionally, physically, financially or sexually. This behavior is typically driven by two distinct mindsets: "conditional love is better than no love at all," or "unconditional love is impossible." Maintaining either mindset positions individuals to accept whatever they can get or nothing at all. The drama that comes with building a marriage based on conditional love is prolonged.

Through seminars and therapy, I have learned that most people just want to be loved for who they are, not for who someone else thinks they are supposed to be. In therapy sessions, clients regularly ask, "Is it too much to ask my partner to just love me for who I am? Is this too difficult?" I often respond, "Unfortunately, it can be challenging and difficult for a lot of us." From birth we are taught that love is conditional. How many times have you heard or made one of the following comments:

- Be successful and I will love you even more.

- I love you, but do not upset me or I will leave.

- You do not have to love individuals who do not love you.

- I am not asking you to change, but if you love me, you will.

- It is difficult for me to love people who act like that.

- Life is about giving and receiving. If you do not give love, do not expect to receive it.

As loving as most people desire to be, the majority do not understand that the comments they make or the behavior they exhibit daily affects their ability and the ability of others to receive and give unconditional love. The problem for most couples is that they have become accustomed to nonsense that they end up looking for it in their marriage. As a child I remember my mother telling me to be careful about what I look for because I just might find it. She went on to say that if you look for trouble, trouble will find you. This is so true! I have discovered that most marriages fail because individuals look for trouble and place limits on how they will give and receive love.

Increased feelings of doubt toward self and others cause individuals to reserve their love until they feel certain that they will not be hurt. However, they fail to realize that life offers no guarantees and those who operate in reserve mode—e.g. "I will not be hurt ever or again"—do not experience unconditional love or live life to the fullest.

In my career, I have yet to meet a woman or man who does not desire to be loved unconditionally. On the contrary, I have met many who desire unconditional love, but do not know how to receive or give it. Dismayed by this unfortunate reality, I began to pay closer attention to the beliefs that women and men embrace about marriage. I found that women and men have different views and expectations about marriage, but share one mutual desire—to receive unconditional love. However, the realization of giving and receiving unconditional love seems impossible at times. False images and portrayals of what "attractive" or "successful" women and men look like continue to penetrate and cloud the minds of millions of good-hearted women and men. Attractive, beautiful and physically fit women and men are idolized. They frequently appear on popular magazine covers, have lead roles in major movies and possess the finer material things in life. Obsession over physical attraction, success, money and fame has caused many individuals to devalue their spouse and walk away from their marriages.

When you think about what you truly desire or have most desired in your current marriage, what comes to mind? What does your checklist of desirable qualities look like? The checklist below is a composite of the top desirable qualities reported by hundreds of individuals with whom I have dialogued with in therapy and social situations.

✓ Someone I can get along with
✓ Someone I can have fun with
✓ Someone who is respectful and trustworthy
✓ Someone who is easy to talk with
✓ Someone who is sexually compatible with me
✓ Someone who is good-looking and physically fit
✓ Someone who shares similar values, interests and goals
✓ Someone who is ambitious and successful
✓ Someone who has a good heart
✓ Someone who is thoughtful
✓ Someone who is spiritual and supportive
✓ Someone who is forgiving and patient
✓ Someone who is financially stable

Is this list familiar to you? Does it represent qualities that you prefer your spouse to possess? Does your spouse possess all or most of the qualities listed above? Did your spouse possess some or all of them initially, but changed?

Obsession over physical attraction, success, money and fame has caused many individuals to devalue their spouse and walk away from their marriage.

After years of providing therapy to couples who could not save their marriages, I decided to examine my list of desirable qualities that I expected my wife to possess and discovered that it resembled the list above. I must say that I was slightly disappointed, but not surprised. After all, I had convinced myself to believe that anyone in their "right" mind would expect their potential mate to have similar qualities. However, after engaging in honest self-reflection, it did not take long for me to figure out that the one quality that I truly desired the most was not on my list. Above and beyond all the other qualities, I, like you, desire to be with someone who will love me unconditionally. Realizing how important this quality is to me, I began to ask myself, why did I exclude it from my list? Was it a conscious or unconscious omission?

As I reflected on my life and the many hardships I have experienced and observed, I concluded at an early age that people cannot love each other unconditionally. This fundamental belief had become entrenched in my emotional reasoning bank. Year after year, I interacted with hundreds of individuals who validated it by displaying conditional love in their relationships. Continually confronted with this reality, I strongly believed that women and men were incapable of loving unconditionally, so I decided to place conditions on how I would love others as well. However, as I matured and acquired spiritual knowledge about healthy relationships, I realized that unconditional love is, in fact, possible, and that my thinking and behavior was bordering on the edge of insanity. Year in and year out I failed to develop unconditional love in my relationships because I believed that I did not have to change how I loved. I continued thinking and behaving in this manner while expecting that unconditional love would somehow surface in my relationships. I knew my *insane* behavior was not effective, but I justified it by telling myself that God knows the condition of my heart. He knows that I "must" have a beautiful woman who possesses all or most of my desirable qualities. I asked myself, "How could I expect anything less if God knows what I desire?" I continued this foolishness for years until I realized that my situation was not changing because the condition of my heart was not right. Let me further explain my dilemma.

Upon meeting my wife, I thought that she was extremely beautiful and physically attractive so I immediately put her in the potential mate category. Sounds shallow right? I agree. Now ask yourself if you did the same with your spouse. The problem with most of us is that our hearts are not centered on what God desires for us, but what we desire for ourselves. I struggled in the beginning phase of my marriage because I chose to love my wife based on conditions (weight, size, appearance, etc.). Finally, being the bright and spiritual man that I am, I realized that my thinking and behavior was incorrect because God does not love based on conditions. This simple yet powerful revelation caused me to re-examine my heart and reevaluate my list of desirable qualities. I eventually came to the realization that I could not depend on my emotions to guide me because they changed based on circumstances or conditions. For example, if I "felt" that my wife was meeting my conditions, I opened up and expressed affection; if I "felt" that my wife was not meeting my conditions, I shut down and withheld affection. I definitely did not understand the meaning of unconditional love and was on a quick path toward divorce.

Filled with discouragement, I asked God to help me discern the difference between love and unconditional love and He did. Through prayer and fellowship with family and friends, I realized that I was placing too much emphasis on qualities that do not endure when adversity and conflict present in marriage.

At moments in our lives we might possess some or all of the qualities listed earlier, but it is too difficult to possess all of them all of the time. Over time our minds and bodies deteriorate and the qualities that we believe to be of importance in the beginning become less important later. This understanding helped me recognize that the only love that will endure when faced with adversity, marital conflict and aging is *unconditional love*.

Over time our minds and bodies deteriorate and the qualities that we believe to be of importance in the beginning become less important later.

The truth is this: no one is perfect! Therefore our qualities change and develop as life throws different challenges our way. Sometimes we're at our best and other times we are not. Are you the kind of person who desires to be with someone who is perfect and is on top of his or her game all the time? If you answered yes, I can relate, but this kind of thinking is irrational and will not allow you to receive or give unconditional love in your marriage. In fact, this kind of thinking creates conditions that are counterproductive to healthy relationships. What do I mean? Let me explain.

Perfection thinking does not allow room or space for errors or flaws in a relationship. If your spouse feels that he or she cannot be him or herself, he or she will experience a great deal of anxiety and the walking on egg-shell syndrome will kick in. Be mindful that no one wants to be in a marriage where they have to watch what they say and do. True harmony occurs in marriage when individuals receive love even when their flaws are visible.

Have you ever wondered why so many people change after they marry? I would argue that most people do not change dramatically, but enter into self-preservation mode until they are comfortable enough to be vulnerable. Conditional love encourages us to walk on eggshells until we think the time is right. Past experiences have taught us that it is inappropriate to "play our vulnerable love card" too soon because we might be hurt and treated unfairly. This is unfortunate because most people truly and sincerely want to give and receive unconditional love in their marriage, but withhold it out of ignorance and fear. Dr. Martin Luther King, Jr. summarized this behavior so gracefully in his statement, "Nothing in the world is more dangerous than sincere ignorance and conscientious stupidity." With this in mind, how long will you continue to sabotage your desire to experience unconditional love in your marriage? Will you continue to live with false hope and miss out on true love because you refuse to change? What's most important to you?

The only love that endures in marriage is unconditional love.

Is it important to you to have a marriage that is built on and sustained with love that is conditional and temporary or a marriage that is built on and sustained with love that is unconditional and permanent? No amount of money, success, ambition, compatibility, eagerness or good intention can give meaning to or sustain your marriage like unconditional love can. By now, I hope you get my point: the only love that endures in marriage is unconditional love.

If you want to learn how to give and receive unconditional love and make your marriage last forever, this book is written specifically for you. The purpose of **Unconditional Love, Marriage Edition** is three-fold: 1) to guide couples who desire to give and receive unconditional love in their marriage, 2) to inspire couples to restore or enhance their marriage based on unconditional love, and 3) to empower couples to make their marriage last forever.

As you continue to read this profound love guide, remember that any love that is worth having is worth working for. *R.E.A.L.* strategies for developing unconditional love in your marriage are provided to empower you, but your ability to benefit from them will require you to work. Start now by opening up your mind and heart.

I've also written a workbook that will help guide you through the chapters of **Unconditional Love, Marriage Edition**. It will help you identify strengths and challenges in regard to giving and receiving unconditional love in your marriage.

I encourage you and your spouse to read this book and complete the workbook together. Keep both books in close vicinity and refer to them regularly. Do not cheat yourself or your spouse out of a loving and lasting marriage. You deserve to receive everything that God has promised, so please stop depriving yourself of the one gift that is priceless and make your marriage last forever: *Unconditional Love*.

PART ONE

UNDERSTANDING LOVE
AND
UNCONDITIONAL LOVE

1

What Is Love
and Why Does It Hurt?

A s I experienced the highs and lows of being in love, I desperately sought answers to two essential questions regarding love's essence and function: "what is love?" and "why does it hurt?" Understanding what love is and how it functions is a prerequisite for developing a marriage that is built on unconditional love. Most women and men struggle to understand the real meaning of love. They also struggle to understand how it works. If you do nothing else in your life, please make time to learn about love.

Knowledge of love and how it works provides a road map for developing healthy self-concepts and marriage. *To live life without love is as harsh as living life without a soul.* Given this, I believe that everyone desires love, but they often don't know what it is or how to get it. In talking with others about the meaning of love, I found that a good number of people agree that love is an emotion of compassion. Some individuals report feelings of exhilaration and excitement when they are in love, while others report strong, intense, and indescribable feelings towards another person. Moreover, a widespread consensus is that love should be untainted.

In my quest to understand and help others to understand what love is and how it functions, I created a definition that encompasses both an emotion and action component. I define love as:

A powerful, compassionate and intangible emotion that directs the hearts of women and men.

Before we move on, let's analyze the three terms I used to create my definition of love. *Powerful* is defined as having great force, power or influence; *Compassionate* is defined as having feelings of mutual respect, trust, and affection; *Intangible* is defined as hard to pin down or identify. Defining love as I did helped me understand individuals' thoughts and behavior more clearly. These three terms can either set the stage for a marriage from heaven or a marriage from hell.

Some say there is a thin line between love and hate. I never understood what this meant, but I do now. The compassion that enables us to love can also enable us to hate when we hurt. The ones we love the most can hurt us the worst. Why? Because we have allowed ourselves to be vulnerable to them and they know exactly what to do to hurt us. They have the power to influence how we give and receive love, thus they also have the ability to influence our hearts and actions.

We do not mind losing power or control of our hearts if we have compassion for someone. If we believe that they will show us mutual respect, trust and affection, we openly allow ourselves to fall in love, thus giving up the ability to control our hearts. As the emotions intensify and the marriage grows, it becomes more difficult to define how we feel. Love becomes intertwined with other emotions and life events. Initially, feelings of delight and happiness consume us and we truly believe that the feeling of love will never go away.

Most conflict in marriage occurs due to hurt emotions, especially when the one emotion that enables us to feel positive regard and affection toward another is hurt: love. As most of us think about love, we associate it with optimistic thinking and positive behavior. Some of us even believe that love conquers all and that our marriage can weather any storm if love is present. At one point in my life I believed this, but not anymore. Not to sound too pessimistic, but I have witnessed too many marriages end in which I was convinced that love was present, although many would question whether love was truly present if the marriage ended.

I disagree and this is why. When individuals feel betrayed, wronged, belittled, unappreciated or disrespected, they lash out emotionally and/or physically in order to protect their heart. People have committed murder and other violent acts out of uncontrollable passion or rage. Conflict occurs and is intensified when compassion is lost or minimized due to internal suffering. Love may still be present during or after the conflict, but most individuals are incapable of expressing it in a compassionate manner when they are hurting.

People have a difficult time coping with being hurt because they believe that love should not hurt. Unfortunately, this flawed thinking causes many to walk away from their marriage because they are hurt. You are probably thinking that if love is supposed to be positive and optimistic, it should not hurt.

Adjust your thinking---love Does Hurt, But not intentionally!

Let me explain why I believe that love hurts! Love hurts because human beings are imperfect. We hurt each other sometimes consciously and sometimes unconsciously. How many times have you heard individuals say, "I love you and did not intend to hurt you"? I defined love as a powerful, compassionate and intangible emotion that directs the heart of women and men. This means that the heart is the control center that manages the emotions that influence our love. In reality, our hearts and emotions, like other things in our lives, change with conditions and circumstances. We withdraw or limit our love when our emotions are hurt, and more often than not, we end up hurting others and ourselves in the process. Although we do not like the pain that is associated with withdrawing or limiting our love, we do so to protect our hearts. The bottom line is that love hurts because we are imperfect and we often engage in self-preserving behavior in order to protect our hearts.

You must realize that love, in and of itself, is not enough to prevent us from hurting each other. Human beings were created out of love to love, but we allow our emotions to distort that love. I suggest that you look at the intent of a person's heart before you eliminate him or her from your life completely. I have learned that good-hearted people say and do bad things when their feelings are hurt. As a result, I try to pay close attention to their underlying motives. If I detect that they are hurting me because they lack insight in expressing their emotions appropriately, I provide support, guidance and prayer. Basically, I stick with them. If I detect that they are deliberately hurting me to be spiteful, I also provide support, guidance and prayer. If the deliberate behavior continues, I simply remove myself from the situation. Adjust your thinking one more time: love does hurt, but not intentionally!

Without question, the essence and function of love is debatable. Due to individual and cultural differences, it is too difficult, if not impossible, to obtain a universal agreement on what love is and how it functions. However, most people would agree that the meaning and application of love can be best clarified by exploring what it is not:

- Love is not hate
- Love is not resentful
- Love is not conditional
- Love is not pride
- Love is not limited
- Love is not a gift from man
- Love is not to be taken for granted
- Love is not restricted to a specific race or gender
- Love is not abuse
- ***Love is not lust***
- Love is not physical, but can be expressed through physical means
- Love is not forced, it is a choice

It is important to understand what love is and is not. Those who fail to learn about love deprive themselves from experiencing true love, and often search for love in all the wrong places and from the wrong people. Comprehending the essence and function of love can help you determine if you should remain in your marriage, as well as help you determine if your marriage is built on and sustained on a solid foundation.

Love Is Not Lust

Marriages that are based on love are more likely to last compared to marriages that are developed out of a strong physical attraction or lust. An issue that continues to astonish me daily is the belief that individuals are capable of falling in love at first sight. I am not sure that this is possible. I do believe that individuals are capable of falling in lust at first sight. Why do I say this? Love is associated with internal attributes (personality, values, the condition of a person's heart, etc.) and lust is associated with physical attributes (nice face, nice butt, sex appeal, etc.). Love requires you to be in a person's presence in order to develop feelings. Lust requires nothing more than a lustful eye. Love develops emotional intimacy, while lust develops physical intimacy that is often mistaken for emotional intimacy. Many individuals build marriages out of lust because they do not understand what real love is. Have you ever listened to a person describe his or her current or potential spouse? How much emphasis is placed on the physical attributes as compared to the internal attributes?

Love is not Lust---*there is a difference!*

Women and men have confused Love with £ust without realizing that they operate in opposition to each other:

L **Love** makes you wait to be married before having sex
L **Lust** makes you jump in bed before marriage

L **Love** enables you to appreciate your significant other's mind
L **Lust** enables you to appreciate your significant other's body

L **Love** makes you yearn for your significant other
L **Lust** makes you yearn for someone else's significant other

L **Love** makes you turn to God and your significant other when trouble is present in your marriage
L **Lust** makes you turn away from God and your significant other when trouble is present in your marriage

L **Love** makes you come home and hold your significant other
L **Lust** makes you stay away from home and hold someone else's significant other

L **Love** contributes to faithfulness
L **Lust** contributes to infidelity

L **Love** enables you to validate, respect and honor your significant other's emotions
L **Lust** contributes to invalidation, disrespect and dishonor

I cannot stress the importance of understanding what love is and how it functions. One cannot remove lust or any other vice from his or her life unless he or she understands what love is. We are living in times when more emphasis is placed on physical qualities and less on internal qualities. This trend is especially dangerous for women and men who define their worth and their spouse's worth by their physical and sexual qualities.

I want to clarify the difference between love and lust because marriages built on love enable individuals to give and receive love. Marriages built on lust cripple individuals and limit their ability to give and receive love. Love does not fade when physical attributes falter, but lust does. Love can repair lust, but lust cannot repair love. Love lasts as long as emotional attraction is strong. Lust lasts as long as physical attraction is strong. What is your marriage built on?

Love = mutual respect, trust and affection: Strong Emotional Intimacy

Lust = one-sided or mutual disrespect, mistrust and detachment: Strong Physical Intimacy

Embrace love and receive all that you can from it, but do not live your life believing that love does not hurt or confusing love with lust! Remember that love is a gift from God. It is a powerful, compassionate and intangible emotion that directs the hearts of women and men. For this reason, love is not to be played with for it can destroy hearts. Now that you have acquired an understanding of what love is, you are one step closer to being able to give and receive the unconditional love that you desire in your marriage. One must first understand what love is before he or she can comprehend the depth and meaning of unconditional love. In the next chapter we will explore what unconditional love is and how it functions.

2

What Is Unconditional Love?

L ike love, the essence and function of unconditional love is debatable and it is too difficult, if not impossible, to obtain a universal agreement on what it is and how it functions. Secular and spiritual counselors have similar thoughts about what unconditional love is and how it functions. Secular counselors refer to unconditional love as being true love between two individuals who love each other regardless of each other's actions or beliefs. Spiritual counselors use the same characterization, but also include forgiveness.

It is my belief that the spiritual definition of unconditional love is most appropriate for individuals who desire to develop relationships that last forever. True forgiveness is required for sincere reconciliation. Many people do not think that unconditional love is possible, but that is because they do not associate it with a Higher Power. Unconditional love is not just about acceptance, it also has a forgiving and nonjudgmental component. God not only accepts us as we are with our imperfections and all, He also forgives us and allows us to redeem ourselves after we engage in inappropriate behavior. He does not withdraw or limit His love. This is the basis of unconditional love. Let me summarize what I believe unconditional love is:

A powerful, compassionate and intangible emotion that directs the hearts of women and men with forgiveness and positive regard.

A thorough comprehension of unconditional love and how it works enables individuals to love others irrespective of the other person's love for them. You can give and receive unconditional love if you learn to address unacceptable behavior without attacking character flaws by withdrawing or limiting your love. As captured in my definition, unconditional love means to forgive and demonstrate positive regard for others.

Forgiveness requires you to remove resentment and anger from your heart in order to develop positive regard for others. Positive regard is a term that was coined by Carl Rogers, a humanistic psychologist who believed that all people have internal resources that are needed to grow. Demonstrating positive regard towards another will enable them to facilitate personal change. Positive regard involves the acceptance of an individual's behaviors and words without judging them. In listening with a non-judgmental attitude you can help individuals see and accept responsibility for their actions. You simply facilitate change, not force it. This is important because most people feel that internal change is more gratifying than external change, and typically lasts longer. Be mindful that we all get annoyed with each other, but, by demonstrating positive regard, we can nurture healthy personal growth. No one likes to be reminded of his or her shortcomings in a negative, judgmental or insensitive manner.

It is imperative that you comprehend what it means to love unconditionally. Your ability to weather storms in your marriage is greatly influenced by your comprehension of unconditional love. Marriages evolve and thrive when individuals love each other unconditionally and understand that their initial attraction is simply a building block—not the key to sustaining their marriage.

So often individuals rely on love to get through tough times, but I would argue that they are relying on the wrong source. Love is a good place to start, but adversity in marriage is conquered with unconditional love. Love is not unconditional love. There is a difference.

*Love is not **Unconditional Love---** there is a difference!*

Most people accept love, but truly desire unconditional love. Love is temporary. Why? Marriages are usually built on love that meets individuals' emotional and physical needs in the interim. As individuals grow in a marriage, they often find that initial love fades. As that initial love fades, the marriage weakens and unconditional love is desired more intensely. While it is true that one cannot achieve unconditional love in their marriage without having some level of love, love does not have the same impact on marriage as unconditional love does. Here's how love and unconditional love differ:

L   **Love** builds marriage

UL   **Unconditional love** sustains them

L   **Love** enables you to remain in your marriage with resentment and anger in your heart

UL   **Unconditional love** enables you to remove resentment and anger from your heart

L   **Love** makes you come home
UL   **Unconditional love** makes you enjoy being at home

L   **Love** feels good most of the time
UL   **Unconditional love** does not always feel good, but is good for you and those you love

L   **Love** is easy to develop and requires little work: a good heart with good intentions
UL   **Unconditional love** is difficult to develop and requires work: a forgiving heart with positive regard for others

L   **Love** is emotionally driven
UL   **Unconditional love** is spiritually driven

L   **Love** evolves through physical proximity, similarities and physical attraction
UL   **Unconditional love** evolves through a relationship with God

The most distinguishing characteristic of unconditional love is that it never fails. Loving unconditionally empowers individuals to accept the bad with the good, and to remain committed to maintaining a joyful and healthy marriage. Unconditional love moves individuals to support each other, work together, and communicate openly with one another.

WHAT IS UNCONDITIONAL LOVE?

Unconditional love sees no limits, feels no limits and accepts no limits.

Your heart can be conditioned to do whatever you want it to do. Why not condition it to love others unconditionally? Unconditional love sees no limits, feels no limits and accepts no limits. If you believe in unconditional love and work to develop it in your marriage, you will reap the benefits of giving and receiving like never before. Sounds simple right? Well it is not. Loving unconditionally is not as easy for some people as it is for others. Why? Just as individuals learn how to walk, talk and eat, they also learn how to love. Understanding why and how you love is critical and will affect how you experience and view marriage from this point on. In the next chapter, *Discover Your Love Style*, I identify the different love styles, explain how they develop and clarify why some people are capable of giving and receiving unconditional love more easily than others.

3

Discover Your Love Style

Are you a conditional lover or an unconditional lover?

U nderstanding your love style is a challenging yet essential task. Knowing how you love will help you cope effectively when faced with adversity in your relationship. Conflict arises in most marriages when one or both individuals feel that they are not being loved unconditionally. The conflict worsens if one or both individuals continually fail to love their significant other in a manner in which he or she desires to be loved. Why does this happen? Excellent question! Unfortunately, many individuals do not understand their own love style. As a result, they struggle to effectively respond to the needs of their significant other as well as their own needs. Lack of knowledge regarding how to love self and others unconditionally is linked to an individual's lack of knowledge about their love style. In order to build a marriage based on unconditional love, you must first understand the two love styles, be able to distinguish one from the other and be aware of how your love style developed. Please allow me to enlighten you.

Conditional Lovers

Conditional lovers give and receive love based on conditions that must be met. This love style is frequently used out of a desire to control one's self or others by limiting or restricting love. Individuals who deploy this love style have a strong need to be in control. Being in control empowers them to master their destiny and minimizes their risk of being vulnerable. Without displaying vulnerability, they avoid the risk of being hurt but also prevent themselves from giving or receiving unconditional love. Receiving and giving motivate conditional lovers, but the fear of pain, suffering and disappointment intensifies their need to receive before giving. An exchange is frequently required. Here are a few examples:

- You respect me and I'll respect you

- You love me unconditionally and I will love you unconditionally

- You talk to me respectfully and I will talk to you respectfully

- You trust me and I will trust you

- You forgive me and I will forgive you

Conditional lovers usually search for and settle down with individuals who have high market value. Physical appearance, wealth, behavior, religious convictions, emotional and intellectual status are gauged by conditional lovers to determine if, how much and when to give love. Their willingness to love unconditionally is strongly influenced by external factors instead of the condition of a person's heart. Individuals who love conditionally often strive to control others: e.g. "If I just give my all, he or she will change," or, "If I enforce my will on him or her I will get what I want." If conditional lovers are not capable of controlling others, they turn their energy inwardly and focus on self. They become high achievers who focus on things that they can control, minimizing their emotional need to be with others, especially individuals they cannot control. This profound need to control one's self and others contributes to feelings of inadequacy, hopelessness, loneliness, helplessness, sadness, anger, greed, bitterness, fear, and even hatred, if efforts to gain control are unsuccessful. Generally speaking, conditional lovers are inpatient and will try to force or control relationship outcomes instead of allowing them to evolve naturally. Engaging in marriage is viewed as a process to be controlled, not experienced. They plant the love seed and then attempt to control how it grows.

Conditional lovers typically practice selfishness, rigidity, and use "I" talk: i.e., I want, I must have and I need. "I" talk is common among conditional lovers. Also be aware that conditional lovers frequently withhold or limit their love based on "standards." Standards are synonymous with conditions. Is this your love style?

Entering into marriage is viewed as a process to be controlled, not experienced. They plant the love seed and then attempt to control how it grows.

Side Note: If you are a conditional lover, please be aware of and try to monitor your conditions or standards. I say this because it is not fair to you or your spouse if you give and receive love based on conditions. People who believe that they have "settled" are typically not happy and will always have a yearning for what they think they are missing. If you married your spouse and he or she does not meet your criteria.... modify your standards and try to learn to love him or her unconditionally.

Unconditional Lovers

Unconditional lovers give and receive love regardless of conditions, even when the return is insufficient or non-reciprocal. What does this mean? We all want something in return right? Yes, but unconditional lovers do not withdraw or restrict their love if the return is insufficient. Individuals who desire to influence others by allowing them to be themselves most frequently use this love style. Individuals who practice this love style rejoice in giving love just as equally as they rejoice in receiving it.

Unconditional lovers allow others to exercise their *free will* because they realize they cannot control others. Additionally, unconditional lovers search for the essence of a person's character and place emphasis on the condition of the person's heart, not their outwardly appearance, achievements or status. Like conditional lovers, unconditional lovers also desire to be with an attractive, smart and financially-stable individual. However, they are more inclined to allow themselves to fall in love with an individual who has an amazing soul. Unconditional lovers are aware that loving unconditionally makes them vulnerable and can potentially cause suffering, but they are also aware that they cannot experience unconditional love unless they allow themselves to be vulnerable. An exchange is not required, but is greatly appreciated. Here are a few examples:

- I respect you and prefer that you respect me

- I love you unconditionally and I hope that you love me the same

- I talk to you respectfully and would appreciate the same consideration

- I trust you, but it is up to you to trust me

- I forgive you and you can choose to forgive me

Unconditional lovers typically search for and settle down with individuals who have average market value, but high market potential. The desire to influence others empowers unconditional lovers to control the things they can control and let go of the things they cannot. This profound understanding of influence contributes to feelings of peace, happiness, calmness, respect, trust, compassion and appreciation, which are manifestations of loving unconditionally. Usually, unconditional lovers are patient. They allow relationship outcomes to evolve naturally instead of trying to force or control them. Engaging in a relationship is viewed by unconditional lovers as a process to be experienced, not controlled. They plant the love seed and allow it to grow without attempting to control it.

Unconditional lovers typically practice selflessness and use "we" talk: i.e., we want, we must have, and we need. "We" talk is common among unconditional lovers. Is this your love style?

Engaging in a relationship is viewed by unconditional lovers as a process to be experienced, not controlled. They plant the love seed and allow it grow without attempting to control it.

Major Distinction Between Conditional and Unconditional Lovers

The major distinction between the two love styles is centered on the intent. Conditional lovers intend to control others' behavior and unconditional lovers intend to influence others' behavior. Conditional lovers attempt to prevent or limit individuals from exercising their *free will* by withdrawing or restricting their love. In contrast, unconditional lovers allow individuals to be themselves without withdrawing or restricting their love. The ability to forgive and show positive regard for others separates unconditional lovers from conditional lovers. Which love style do you prefer?

How Do Love Styles Develop?

The way in which we give and receive love can be best understood by exploring the three most influential factors that affect our beliefs and actions about receiving and giving love: family teachings or observations, previous relationship experiences, and societal perceptions.

Family Teachings or Observations

If you desire to learn how an individual's love style developed, simply inquire about his or her childhood experiences. We are all by-products of our total life experiences, including childhood experiences. Too often, children are taught directly or indirectly that love must be reciprocal. As a result they struggle to love themselves and others when they do not feel loved.

Our first exposure to interpersonal relationships comes from family interactions. Through direct involvement or observation we learn certain skills and habits, including how to receive and give love. Regardless of the method, we initially develop love styles from our family members. Most individuals would like to think that they love the way they do based on personal experiences alone, but this is not true. We have all been impacted by family experiences in some form or fashion.

Children who grow up in households where love is expressed freely and without hesitation are likely to become adults who express love freely and without hesitation. The process of learning how to give and receive love is strongly influenced by the adults in a child's life. For example, if a child witnesses his or her parent express love when he or she is pleased or happy, the child may learn that love is shared only under pleasant conditions or circumstances. On the other hand, if a child witnesses his or her parent express love when he or she is dissatisfied or unhappy, the child may learn that love is shared regardless of conditions or circumstances.

If an individual is abused, observes abuse, receives inadequate love or is deprived of love during their childhood, it is highly likely that he or she will be emotionally guarded as an adult. Some clients I have worked with, who have experienced abuse in their childhood, have expressed difficulty with receiving and giving love unconditionally. Others developed poor boundaries and expressed that they often give too much of themselves to compensate for the love they did not receive in their childhood. For many, childhood experiences have taught them that one must guard their heart to prevent suffering or love freely to experience the benefits of loving unconditionally.

Different love styles can potentially cause conflict in marriage because individuals from different backgrounds frequently experience and express love differently. Discussions about childhood upbringing can provide vital information about the development of an individual's love style. The behaviors and customs that individuals present in adulthood were shaped over a period of time. Understanding their foundation is vital to having a clear picture of how they give and receive love.

> *Different love styles can potentially cause conflict in marriage because individuals from different backgrounds frequently experience and express love differently.*

Examples:

Jimmy: "My childhood was okay. My parents' marriage was good and bad. When they were happy with each other the house was filled with love. However, when they were unhappy or angry with each other the house was filled with tension. If my mother was upset with my father she made him sleep on the couch and spoke harshly to him; if my father was upset with my mother he was mean to her and attempted to limit her independence. I assumed they placed these conditions on each other in an attempt to control behavior. From my childhood experience, I learned to give love during positive situations and limit love during negative or tense situations. In my current marriage, I often find myself expressing love when I am in a good mood or happy. I never assumed that my childhood experience had such an effect on how I give and receive love. I guess I learned to love based on conditions."

Conditional Lover or Unconditional Lover?

Michele: "My parents had disagreements like any other couple. My father was not happy with my mother's frequent shopping sprees. They fought and argued frequently, but their love for each other did not alter. My father told me that he learned early in life that people cannot be controlled. He was upset with my mother and wanted her to stop shopping, but did not outwardly express his frustration or limit his love. Instead he sat down with my mother, reviewed bank statements with her and expressed how he felt. He helped her understand that her spending habits were negatively affecting their ability to plan for the future. My mother told me that it was difficult to stop spending money freely, but she worked hard because my father did not try to control her. She appreciated that he was patient with her and did not place conditions on her. From my childhood experience, I learned that it is best to try to influence others' behavior. Love has nothing to do with controlling others."

Conditional Lover or Unconditional Lover?

Previous Relationship Experiences

Childhood experience may strongly influence one's love style, but it does not solely determine it. Through relationships with others as adults, the love style we developed in childhood can be sustained or altered. Positive and healthy past relationships contribute to an individual's willingness to express love unconditionally and without fear. However, negative and unhealthy past relationships can contribute to an individual's unwillingness to express love unconditionally.

Past failed relationships may have long-term negative effects on individuals if they lack healthy coping skills. A damaged heart and loss of trust is difficult to repair. Some individuals learn and grow in a positive manner from failed relationships, while others become victims who allow pain and suffering to destroy their desire to give and receive unconditional love. Seeking to understand an individual's previous relationship experiences can offer useful information in regards to understanding his or her love style.

Examples:

June: "I was married for ten years and gave my all to my husband. I do not know why my husband left. Some people can't appreciate anything or anyone. I am not giving my all again. Whomever I date in the future will have to work really hard to earn my love. My previous pain reminds me of the importance of shielding my heart from others. My friends tell me that I will never find true love by doing so, but I do not care."

Conditional Lover or Unconditional Lover?

Sam: "My relationship with my ex-wife did not work, but I enjoyed our time together. Over the course of our five-year marriage we learned that we were different. Her values were different than mine and we argued too much. We loved each other, but could not make it work. I gave what I thought was my all, but apparently it was not enough to save my marriage. It hurt me really bad to see my marriage end, but I am not afraid to love again. I forgave my wife for everything she did to me and prayed that she would forgive me for the things I did to her."

Conditional or Unconditional Lover?

Societal Perceptions

Societal perceptions regarding how women and men should love also contribute to the development of love styles. Women are perceived to be sensitive individuals who are expected to sacrifice their happiness to please others. In contrast, men are perceived to be sensitively-challenged individuals who are expected to put their needs before others. Throughout history, both women and men have accepted these perceptions as fact. It is unfortunate that such perceptions penetrate to the core of our society. Child-rearing and adult relationships are influenced by these societal views. Given the differences in perceptions, one would assume that, in comparison to men, women are more likely to embrace unconditional love as their love style. Over the course of my career as a therapist I have witnessed thousands of women do whatever they can to give and receive love, even putting others' needs before their own. In fact, women initiated eighty-five percent of the couple's therapy sessions I have conducted. I make this distinction not to say that women cannot be conditional lovers, but to point out that women are more likely to embrace characteristics of an unconditional lover. Understanding your love style also requires an understanding of societal perceptions. Furthermore, if you desire to learn more about your significant other's love style, explore his or her ideas about how women and men love, and compare them to societal perceptions.

Now that you have a bettering understanding of different love styles and how they develop, do you feel good about your love style? You cannot change your childhood experiences, past relationships or societal perceptions, but you can change your love style. If you are a conditional lover and would like to transform into an unconditional lover, there are two key strategies to follow:

1.) Establish a relationship with God.

    a.   God will bless you with knowledge and wisdom that will enhance your understanding of the true meaning of unconditional love. He gave his only begotten son so that you can have a second chance at life and love. Redemption was granted not by your doing, but by the compassion and grace of God. Study the *Word* and learn to do what God has already done for you.

2.) Treat others as you would like to be treated – this is the Golden Rule.

    a.   If you desire to be loved unconditionally, learn what it takes to love others unconditionally and strive to treat others the way you expect to be treated. You may struggle to relate to others at times, but put yourself in their shoes and respond to them in the same manner you would want or expect them to respond to you.

A lack of understanding about different love styles can lead to an unproductive and unhappy marriage. You need to be aware of your love style and be willing to modify it if you desire to have a marriage filled with unconditional love. Combining your new knowledge with strategies you will learn in the following chapters will guide the course of your marriage for years to come. In the second section of this book, I present R.E.A.L. strategies that you should master in order to be successful at giving and receiving unconditional love in your marriage.

PART TWO

HOW TO GIVE AND RECEIVE UNCONDITIONAL LOVE IN YOUR MARRIAGE

4

The R.E.A.L. Concept

In previous chapters I defined love and unconditional love, and discussed their functions. I also defined love styles and how they develop. This chapter provides you with a concept that will empower you to apply the knowledge you have acquired about unconditional love. Proper knowledge about love is paramount in having a healthy marriage. However, possessing knowledge is not beneficial unless it can be applied in your marriage. To assist you with this undertaking, I developed the R.E.A.L. concept and have found it instrumental in helping individuals give and receive unconditional love.

The R.E.A.L. Concept

Each relationship is distinct and has its own unique challenges. The R.E.A.L. concept can be used as a tool to help you understand what unconditional love is and how to develop it in your relationship. The R.E.A.L. concept is articulated as:

R – *Realistic* approach
E – Rational **E***xpectations*
A – Positive *Attitude*
L – *Love* unconditionally

The "R"

The R encourages you to approach situations in a *Realistic* manner. It is important to express an awareness of things as they really are but also to use sound judgment and demonstrate empathy. Also seek to understand the source of problems before you attempt to address or solve them.

The "E"

The E encourages you to exercise sound reasoning in order to develop rational *Expectations* or beliefs. The expectations you have of yourself, others and life in general often reflect how you live your life. Eliminate irrational expectations and replace them with rational ones.

The "A"

The A encourages you to maintain a positive *Attitude* of yourself and others. Do not let your attitude or feelings prevent you from being happy or progressing in life. Negativity begets negativity. Change starts with you.

The "L"

The L encourages you to develop unconditional *Love* for yourself and others. Establish a deep, tender, indefinable feeling of affection and attentiveness toward yourself and others that is not determined or influenced by someone or something.

This concept provides a road map for giving and receiving unconditional love in your marriage. There can't be unconditional love in any relationship without the development and application of appropriate and healthy interpersonal skills. The R.E.A.L. approach is the best method for giving and receiving unconditional love. It encourages women and men to interact with each other in a respectful, empathic, nonjudgmental and positive manner.

The concept can be essential to saving and restoring a troubled relationship, but the successful application of the concept requires individuals to be intellectually and emotionally balanced. In order to approach situations realistically and develop rational expectations, you must be capable of thinking clearly and objectively. Additionally, to maintain a positive attitude and develop unconditional love, you must be capable of feeling wholeheartedly and subjectively. Giving and receiving unconditional love is possible if you use the R.E.A.L. concept, but be aware of self-preserving personality traits that can prevent and limit you from using the concept successfully in your marriage.

SELF-PRESERVING PERSONALITY TRAITS

At points in our lives we rely on certain personality traits more than others, and learn to use traits that are common to us or appear to reap the greatest benefit for us. I have observed that one or two distinctive, but domineering, self-preserving personality traits primarily drive both women and men: "The Emotional Me Trait" or "The Intellectual Me Trait."

The Emotional Me Trait

The "Emotional Me Trait" is an expressive trait that enables individuals to communicate how they feel. The trait receives fuel from the heart and is mainly operated by feelings. Individuals who utilize this trait frequently, often believe that feelings are as equally important, or more important, than facts. Subjectivity or emotionality play a vital role in how they make decisions and experience life.

Expressing sensitive and nurturing emotions and giving of self freely is valued, encouraged and praised. However, individuals who are dominated by this personality trait have difficulty understanding and connecting reason and emotion. Their emotions either block or limit their ability to view or comprehend things rationally. They speak and behave based on how they feel. Their intellectual capacity is not necessarily inadequate, but is dominated by emotions. They will endure prolonged suffering to preserve their "Emotional Me Trait."

The "Emotional Me Trait" has created emotional distress and confusion for many women and men. I have personally witnessed individuals engage in demoralizing and self-inhibiting behavior in an attempt to preserve their "Emotional Me Trait." For example: remaining in emotionally and/or physically abusive relationships because they would "feel" bad if they walked away, and refusing to seek help because they "feel" they can resolve their own problem or would "feel" bad if someone knew their marriage was troubled. This profound desire to preserve and nurture the "Emotional Me Trait" has proven to be detrimental to women and men's emotional and physical health.

Women and men have a deep need to be loved, especially unconditionally, and will often accept and tolerate "nonsense" in their marriage as long as they "feel" loved. The "Emotional Me Trait" occasionally prevents women and men from approaching situations in a *Realistic* manner and developing rational *Expectations*. This, in turn, contributes to their inability to apply the R.E.A.L. concept successfully in their marriage.

The Intellectual Me Trait

The "Intellectual Me Trait" is a thought-provoking trait that enables individuals to communicate what they think. The trait receives fuel from the psyche and is mainly operated by intellect. Individuals who utilize this trait frequently, often believe that facts are as equally important or more important than emotions. Objectivity or impartiality play a vital role in how they make decisions and experience life. Expression of sensitive and nurturing emotions and giving freely of self is calculated and executed with apprehension and foresight. Individuals who are dominated by this personality trait have difficulty understanding and connecting emotion and reason. Their intellect either blocks or limits their ability to view or comprehend things emotionally. They speak and behave based on how they think. Their emotional capacity is not necessarily inadequate, but is dominated by intellect.

The "Intellectual Me Trait" enables individuals to guard their hearts from emotional pain. However, it also contributes to the emotional distance that usually manifests in their marriage. I have personally witnessed individuals engage in inappropriate verbal confrontations in an attempt to preserve their "Intellectual Me Trait." They rely heavily on their intellect to cope with and understand life challenges. If they are forced to deal with emotions, they are likely to become frustrated when their intellect fails them. Individuals who rationalize everything typically have difficulty feeling wholeheartedly and subjectively, thus causing others to categorize them as negative individuals who do not love unconditionally.

The "Intellectual Me Trait" can prevent women and men from maintaining a positive *Attitude* and developing unconditional *Love* if they fail to understand or comprehend something intellectually. This in turn contributes to their inability to apply the R.E.A.L. concept successfully in their marriage.

To bond with and express unconditional love for your significant other, it is necessary that you understand *love styles* highlighted in Chapter Three and *self-preserving personality traits* highlighted above. In doing so, you can gain insight that will help you cope with differences between you and your partner more effectively. As mentioned in Chapter Three, love styles are developed based on family teachings or observations, previous relationship experiences and societal views. The same factors also influence the development of self-preserving personality traits as well. Similar to your love style, your self-preserving personality trait strongly influences how you express love.

During my investigation on how to help women and men give and receive unconditional love, I discovered that love styles and self-preserving personality traits definitely affect how individuals give and receive unconditional love. I also discovered that there are two categories of conditional lovers and two categories of unconditional lovers. Let's look at each category.

Intellectual Conditional Lover (ICL)
Versus
Emotional Conditional Lover (ECL)

Intellectual Conditional Lover (ICL)

You give and receive love based on intellectual aptitude. You need to be stimulated intellectually or you lose interest. Intelligence is very appealing and attractive to you. You will give love if your significant other meets your intellectual need. However, if your significant other is not capable of intellectualizing like yourself, you withdraw or limit your love to protect your heart.

Emotional Conditional Lover (ECL)

You give and receive love based on emotional aptitude. You need to be stimulated emotionally or you lose interest.

You will share your emotions freely as long as you are receiving what you put out. However, if your significant other is incapable of meeting your emotional needs, you withdraw or limit your love to protect your heart.

Intellectual Unconditional Lover (IUCL)
Versus
Emotional Unconditional Lover (EUCL)

Intellectual Unconditional Lover (IUCL)

You give and receive love based on intellectual aptitude, but do not withdraw or limit your love if your significant other is not capable of doing the same. You search for commonalities and learn to appreciate your significant other for who he or she is. You strive to enhance your significant other's intellectual capacity, but do not force him or her to view the world through your intellectual lens.

Emotional Unconditional Lover (EUCL)

You give and receive love based on emotional aptitude, but do not withdraw or limit your love if your significant other is not capable of doing the same. You explore options to help him or her comprehend the importance of good emotional health. You understand that emotions are expressed in a variety of ways and strive to expand your understanding of your significant other's emotional "intelligence" while nurturing your emotional needs.

If you and your significant other are experiencing ongoing conflict over what appear to be trivial and solvable issues, it may be that you do not understand each other's dominate self-preserving personality trait or love style.

Comprehension of the self-preserving traits outlined in this chapter, along with comprehension of love styles, can help you better understand how you and your significant other express love and cope with adversity differently in your marriage. Depending on what is happening in your relationship and your comfort level, you might rely heavily on one trait. However, to successfully apply the concept in your marriage you must learn to balance both traits. God created humans, both women and men, with the ability to "feel" and "think" because He understood the importance of balance. As the saying goes, too much of anything is not healthy. There is a time to think, a time to feel and a time to do both.

Allowing one of the two self-preserving personality traits to dominate you is not beneficial for you or your significant other. If your dominant trait is different than your significant other, make time to learn about his or her trait and practice incorporating it into your marriage. Don't ignore, minimize or attempt to change it. Learning to balance the expression of self-preserving personality traits is a critical skill that will enable you to succeed in most tasks, including the implementation of this empowering concept in your marriage. In the remaining chapters, you will learn how to balance your self-preserving personality traits and apply the R.E.A.L. Concept to develop and sustain the unconditional love you desire.

5

Strategy #1:

Be Realistic

Relationships Are 1 Percent Love and 99 Percent Work

Most people enter into marriage with the intent of living happily ever after, but do not realize or want to accept the fact that relationships are 1 percent love and 99 percent work. You are probably saying that no marriage can last forever if love plays such a small role. I previously thought the same thing, but have learned otherwise. If love alone was enough to maintain relationships, the divorce rate would not be at 50 percent and climbing. Marriage does not endure because of love, but because of the work that is invested to nurture love. The ability to give and receive unconditional love requires you to take action. If you learn nothing else about relationships, remember that they are 1 percent Love and 99 percent Work.

Relationships Are 1 Percent Love

The exhilarating feeling of being in love typically lasts eighteen months to two years, a time period in which most relationship experts refer to as the "honeymoon stage."

During this timeframe individuals go out of their way to please each other. Apologizing for mistakes is common, just as gifts and surprises for birthdays and anniversaries come without reminders or requests. "I Love You" is repeated numerous times throughout the day and even in the presence of others. Physical and emotional affection is abundant. Sexual encounters are spontaneous, exciting and viewed as mind-blowing because the heart is well positioned.

Thoughts of being with the other person run rampantly through individuals' minds daily. "I am so in love with you" is said with enthusiasm. No wrongs are worth arguing over during this time period. Difficult-to-cope-with qualities such as stubbornness and inflexibility are minimized or are addressed in a positive and patient manner. Personality and value differences are viewed as strengths instead of obstacles. Individuals often state, "Where I am weak, you are strong. This is why our marriage is so wonderful." Loving each other unconditionally seems effortless, and individuals question why they waited so long to feel so good.

The couple is soaring off of love and does not want to do anything to ruin their high. Love rules the marriage and feelings of inseparability are enough to persuade both individuals to support each other through the good and bad. Does any of this sound familiar? Everything that happens during this period strongly contributes to the 1 percent of love that exists in most marriages.

The exhilarating feeling of being in Love typically lasts eighteen months to two years.

Relationships Are 99 Percent Work

Love without work does not last. After the exhilarating feeling of being in love weakens, reality sets in and the dynamics of being in a committed marriage—including building and maintaining a life together, adjusting to career shifts, parental responsibilities, occasional in-law dilemmas and life stressors in general—begin to take a toll on the marriage. Now, individuals attempt to balance personal needs with their mate's needs, but find it difficult to do so at times. The hustle and bustle that comes with trying to secure and maintain the American dream and keeping a spouse, two kids and a dog happy, leaves little time to express physical, sexual and emotional affection. Sexual encounters are scheduled, not as exciting and viewed as part of marital obligation. Complacency sets in and "I Love You is *replaced* with "You know I love you, I should not have to say it all the time."

Difficult-to-cope-with qualities such as stubbornness and inflexibility are seen as such and are typically addressed in a negative or belittling manner. Personality and value differences are viewed as obstacles instead of strengths. Individuals often state, "We are so different and this is why we have so many problems in our marriage." Striving to love each other unconditionally is exhausting and leads some to question why they rushed to get married. Depending on the intensity and number of stressors in the relationship, one or both individuals might say, "I love you, but I am not in love with you anymore."

Love is still present, but is slowly fading. Thoughts of the marriage ending influence both individuals to do what is best for themselves. Both individuals realize that work is needed if the marriage is to survive. Does this sound familiar? Everything that happens during this period accounts for the 99 percent of work that is required to maintain most marriages.

Love without work does not last.

Now that I have explained my theory, let's test your knowledge about relationships. Answer the true and false questions below.

1) Good intentions with poor communication can sustain a marriage. True or False

2) If love is present in marriage, work is not needed. True or False

3) Love only fades when serious problems are present in marriage. True or False

4) People maintain happy marriages by working to satisfy each other. True or False

5) Any marriage worth having is worth working for. True or False

Continue reading for the answers.

Why Is It Important to Comprehend the 1 Percent Love - 99 Percent Work Relationship Theory?

It is important for individuals to be aware of what typically happens in marriage from beginning to end. Bad marriages usually do not occur overnight. Generally speaking, a large percentage of relationships fail due to a lack of work, not love. Love is definitely needed in any relationship that will endure for any period of time; however, love is simply an emotion that has no meaning unless something is done to sustain it. My 1% Love and 99% Work Relationship Theory was derived from sessions with married couples. In session after session, I would hear women and men say that marriage requires a great deal of work, even happy marriages. To better understand the reason why so many couples feel this way, I began to track and document their responses. The results revealed the following:

1) Women and men view marriage and committed relationships as social institutions that require individuals to cooperate or comply with certain rules or expectations. Each individual enters marriage with pre-set core values or standards that define appropriate and inappropriate behavior. Value differences are either unrecognized or ignored in the beginning of most marriages because individuals believe that value differences should not be problematic for individuals who are deeply in love. Well, these differences can be problematic. Why?

2) Unfortunately, a large percentage of individuals who get married do not share similar *core values* or *are not willing to work to establish them*. Values are traits that are considered worthwhile and represent an individual's highest priorities and deeply held driving forces. Value differences in marriage mean that additional work is necessary to coexist in harmony.

Do you have friends or family members who are experiencing difficulty in their marriages because of value differences?

Establishing and maintaining relationships is fundamental to human existence. Relationships enable individuals to bond with others and fulfill their need for intimacy. The need to grow and connect with another person is the primary reason why most of us marry. Unfortunately, we enter marriage with individuals only to find out later that their core values are completely different than ours. How and why does this happen? It is usually due to physical proximity, similarities and physical attractiveness. Let's review all three.

Physical proximity is important because as humans we have a tendency to bond with individuals who are physically close to us. Familiarity and opportunity are underlying motives for establishing relationships based on physical proximity. The more you are around a person, the more the person is likely to "grow" on you. Frequent contact can enhance positive feeling toward another individual.

Next, similarities are also influential in determining whether one will enter into a relationship. You bond with individuals that appear to share similar goals, entertainment and social preferences, and beliefs as yourself. Similarity helps individuals feel comfortable and reduces distress and tension. For example, individuals typically report the following: "We like to do the same things. We go out to eat, socialize with friends, dance, travel, etc." However, when asked about similarities in regard to communicating, respect and trust, individuals usually express significant differences.

Lastly, physical attraction is the third reason someone decides to enter into a relationship. Individuals are initially attracted to others based on their physical appearance. This is very prevalent in our society because physical attractiveness is rewarded. Individuals who are very attractive are usually popular and receive more attention than less attractive people.

While all three reasons factor significantly in the decision to enter into marriage, I believe that a relationship will be troubled if core values are not similar. When getting to know an individual, physical attraction and proximity set the stage. Physical attraction initially influences your desire to approach another person and physical proximity gives you an opportunity to meet and interact with him or her. If you discover that the other person has similar interests, you are encouraged to pursue the relationship. Similarities set the stage for intimate relationships to develop. Individuals who appear to share similar interests and beliefs, are more likely to enter into an intimate relationship. However, dissimilarity in core values will cause conflict. I have provided counseling to hundreds of couples who were troubled because they did not share similar core values about communication, money management, expression of emotions and other issues that affect the quality of marriages. Interpersonal similarities are needed to develop a relationship, but similar core values are needed to sustain it.

Many individuals marry because of physical attraction and superficial similarities, but give little thought to the importance of sharing similar core values. In my opinion, the ability to give and receive unconditional love is easier for individuals who share similar core values or are willing to develop them. If physical attraction and superficial similarities were enough, individuals would have long and prosperous relationships and the institute of marriage would not be in jeopardy. However, this is not the case. The marriage institution is steadily eroding because physical appearance and superficial similarities are being used as foundational cornerstones. Because values influence your behavior, it is important that you work to develop similar core values with your spouse. Make sure that your core values are compatible with his or hers. No other social institution is affected by the lack of similarities in core values like the institute of marriage. The best marriages have two individuals who are dedicated to working and developing similar core values.

Many individuals marry because of physical attraction and superficial similarities, but give little thought to the importance of sharing similar core values.

The Marriage Institution

Marriage is a beautiful union and can bring a wealth of joy if the "right" kind of work is conducted to sustain it. In the past two years, I have attended four weddings and experienced mixed feelings each time I heard the minister facilitate the exchange of vows. One side of me was filled with gladness and optimism while the other side was filled with sadness and pessimism. On one occasion, I questioned whether both individuals truly understood the seriousness of what they had just agreed to. The exchange occurred as follows:

Minster: Do you, John Williams, take Susan Johnson to be your wife – to live together after God's ordinance – in the holy estate of matrimony? Will you love her, comfort her, honor and keep her, in sickness and in health, for richer, for poorer, for better, for worse, in sadness and in joy, to cherish and continually bestow upon her your heart's deepest devotion, forsaking all others, keeping yourself only unto her as long as you both shall live?

John Williams: I will.

Minster: Do you, Susan Johnson, take John Williams to be your husband – to live together after God's ordinance – in the holy estate of matrimony? Will you love him, comfort him, honor and keep him, in sickness and in health, for richer, for poorer, for better, for worse, in sadness and in joy, to cherish and continually bestow upon him your heart's deepest devotion, forsaking all others, keeping yourself only unto him as long as you both shall live?

Susan Johnson: I will.

After hearing the vows, my joyful and optimistic side was convinced that love and good intention would help the couple remain committed to their vows. On the other hand, my worried and pessimistic side was convinced that love alone will not help the couple remain committed to their vows. As I explored my ambivalence, I realized that I felt pessimism because I had conversed and interacted with hundreds of individuals who had repeated the same vows, only to walk away from the marriages when things were not going well.

In my experience as a therapist, I have found that individuals find it easy to love and honor their spouse when they are healthy, financially stable, and joyful. However, I have found that the same individuals restrict or limit their love, and dishonor their spouse when they are sick, financially or emotionally unstable or experience periods of sadness. For this reason, I do not think that love alone is enough to help individuals remain committed to their vows. When things get rough, as they will, love and a working attitude must be present to sustain the marriage.

Marriage vows were written with a function component that addresses the good and bad in marriage. I believe they were written as they are to remind individuals that relationships require work. It is frequently said that individuals work for what they want. Unfortunately, this exemplary work ethic appears to apply to every aspect of life except in intimate personal relationships. It saddens me to see how easily individuals move from marriage to marriage when they are unhappy. Marriages, like other social institutions, grow and prosper when individual team players are committed to investing quality time and energy into preserving it.

I will provide a parallel example to further demonstrate my point. The military has endured much turmoil for several decades but has had much success in motivating individuals to remain committed to the institution. How? As individuals enter the military they are required to take an oath. The oath, like a marriage vow, is a commitment to the institution and reads as follows:

I, _____, do solemnly swear (or affirm) that I will support and defend the Constitution of the United States against all enemies, foreign and domestic; that I will bear true faith and allegiance to the same; that I take this obligation freely, without any mental reservation or purpose of evasion; and that I will well and faithfully discharge the duties of the office on which I am about to enter. So help me God.

While many claim to understand the meaning of their marriage vows, many fail to uphold them during difficult times. Similar to the military oath, marriage vows provide the framework for expected and desired behavior of members in the institution. In order to preserve the institution, unity and harmony must be present. What does this mean and how can it be accomplished?

During rough times in their marriages, individuals frequently engage in behavior that will potentially advance their personal interests, thus causing disharmony in the institution. This self-preserving behavior is a natural response to disorderliness, but often places personal interests above what is important to preserving the institution. Selfish and self-centered behavior is the primary reason for the failure of most marriages. So in order to preserve the institution, behavior must be consistent and have shared significance to each member in the institution. This is referred to as "harmonizing" and can be accomplished by establishing core values.

Military leaders realized that the oath alone, like marriage vows is too difficult to uphold during difficult times. Thus, core values were designed to guide the behavior of all members in the institution. Core values inspire each member to do his or her best to preserve the institution and remind individuals of their commitment when faced with adversity. Core values are constant when everything is wavering and changing. As a member of the United States Air Force for nearly a decade, I can attest that I learned to appreciate the importance of core values such as: Integrity First, Service Before Self and Excellence in All We Do. I believe that you can apply these core values in your marriage and experience the uniformity and connectivity that the military has sustained and enjoyed for decades. Let's explore this further.

Integrity First – means to act in a righteous manner even when no one is looking. A person of integrity is honest, courageous, responsible, open, humble, accountable and respectful of self.

- **Honest:** your word is your bond. Lying is not an option.
- **Courageous:** you do what is right even if the cost is high.
- **Responsible:** you accept your duties and perform them responsibly.
- **Open:** you seek feedback to ensure you are performing your duties satisfactorily.
- **Humble:** you embrace your duties with humility and strive to do your best.
- **Accountable:** you accept responsibility for your actions and do not take credit for others.
- **Self-respect:** you behave in a manner that will not harm the reputation of self.

A person of integrity will uphold their marriage vows, walk away from adulterous sexual advances or opportunities, accept his or her duties as a husband or wife, solicit feedback from their spouse or others in order to perform his or her duties satisfactorily, remain humble, accept responsibility for his or her actions and respect self at all times.

An individual of integrity is honest, courageous, responsible, open, humble, accountable and respectful of self.

Service Before Self – means that one is willing to put his or her personal goals or desires on hold or adapt goals that will satisfy self-interests and advance the goals of the institution.

- **Selflessness:** you do what is best for the betterment of the institution, not just the self.
- **Flexible:** you learn to incorporate personal goals into selfless goals that strengthen the institution, not weaken it.
- **Discipline and in Control:** you do not indulge in self-pity, anger, discouragement, frustration or defeatism. You lead with an optimistic attitude and mindset.

A person who embraces service before self will not allow his or her pride or personal agenda prevent him or her from doing what is best for his or her marriage; he or she will seek opportunities to strengthen his or her marriage by incorporating personal goals with marital goals; he or she gives because it is the right thing to do, not because there is a return; finally, he or she accepts life challenges without feeling sorry for self, displaying anger, frustration, discouragement or defeatism. He or she embraces what it means to compromise, but also realizes that he or she will have to occasionally sacrifice to preserve the institution.

> *An individual who embraces service before self is willing to put his or her personal goals or desires on hold or adapt goals that satisfy self-interests and advance the marriage.*

Excellence in All We Do – means to develop or maintain a passion for continuous growth and improvement that will drive the institution into a long-term, upward spiral of achievement and performance.

- **Personal excellence:** you engage in activities that will enhance your spiritual, physical and mental capabilities.
- **Mutual respect:** you treat others with respect regardless of their attributes.

A person who embraces excellence in all we do constantly looks for opportunities to improve his or her marriage and self; he or she believes that complacency and mediocrity is unacceptable; he or she welcomes challenges and problems as opportunities to excel; finally, he or she understands that each person is unique and can contribute if guided correctly.

> *An individual who embraces Excellence in All We Do develops or maintains a passion for continuous growth and improvement that will drive the marriage into a long-term, upward spiral of achievement and performance.*

On the day that you recite your marriage vows, you have a strong desire to do what is right and hope that your union will last forever. You feel that your struggles are a thing of the past and that love will propel your relationship to the next level. However, a lack of compatible core values will destroy or create distress in your marriage. If you desire to give and receive unconditional love in your marriage, work to establish similar core values if they do not already exist.

Values form the foundation for everything that happens in your relationships. Whatever values you hold will inundate your relationship. You will experience continued hardship if your values differ significantly from your significant other. If you are generally happy in your marriage, you probably selected a spouse who shares core values that are congruent with your own. Conversely, if you're not happy in your marriage, watch for dissimilarity between what you value and what your spouse values. Be mindful that no two individuals are the same. There are no perfect matches, and love, like anything else in life, is expressed differently and shifts based on circumstances. Be realistic and prepare to work in order to give and receive the unconditional love you desire in your marriage. Seek to understand the source of your relational conflict, then use sound judgment and demonstrate empathy to address it. If you desire to give and receive unconditional love, you have to devote time and energy—***work at it!***

6

Strategy #2:

Develop Rational Expectations

"Expectations Guide Behavior"

eveloping rational expectations is the second strategy that will enable you to give and receive unconditional love in your marriage. What you expect from your marriage is typically what you give. The expectations you have of yourself and others often reflect how you behave in your relationship. Did you enter into marriage hoping to receive unconditional love, but had no intention of truly giving it? Did you expect your spouse to love you for who you are, but you put on a façade because of personal shortcomings or flaws? Did you enter into marriage thinking that love will conquer all? If you answered yes, you need to evaluate your expectations. Evaluating your expectations is critical in being able to give and receive unconditional love. Expectations are powerful and can predispose you to certain experiences. Irrational expectations often cause or contribute to inappropriate expression of emotions and behavior. While rational expectations often cause or contribute to appropriate expression of emotions and behavior. You should make every effort to learn the difference. Let's review.

Expect to Give

Give is an action verb, which means to put into the possession of another for his or her use. For God so loved the world that He gave His only begotten Son, that whoever believes in Him should not perish, but have eternal life (John 3:16). Some people are takers and some are givers. What kind of person are you? Do you give with a cheerful heart or out of obligation or guilt? Individuals who give with a cheerful heart understand the value of giving and the meaning of "Reap What You Sow." If you give conditional love, you will most likely receive conditional love. However, if you give unconditional love, you will almost certainly receive unconditional love.

Individuals who give with a cheerful heart understand the value of giving and the meaning of "Reap What You Sow."

It is irrational to expect to receive unconditional love if you are not willing to give it. If you are a Christian, I hope that you strive to give unconditional love like God does. No marriage can survive if only one person is giving. We all have a desire to receive, but routinely place too much emphasis on receiving and fail to appreciate the power of giving. Giving empowers you. Do not focus on the return because you cannot control what it will be. Instead give unconditional love and pray that it influences others to do the same.

Expect to Accept Your Significant Other for Who They Are

Entering into marriage and expecting to change your significant other will cause more problems in your marriage than you can ever imagine. Understand that most people just want to be accepted for who they are. Attempts to change others frequently contribute to feelings of resentment and bitterness. Recognize that what you believe is right for someone does not matter unless they agree. This is important to understand, because you must realize that change will not occur or last unless your significant other can identify with the requested change and personally embrace it. If individuals are persuaded to do things they do not have a desire to do, they will most likely grow resentful or bitter, especially if the outcome does not meet their expectations. I realize that it is difficult to accept individuals as they are, especially when flaws are visible and appear to be destructive or self-inhibiting. However, individuals are more open to change if they feel that they are accepted despite their shortcomings.

True acceptance means to acknowledge positive and negative traits. A quick way to distance yourself from your significant other is to embrace his or her strengths and complain about his or her weaknesses. Have you ever observed how quickly your mood shifts after someone tells you that you are not good at something or they do not offer positive support? If you do not agree with or dislike something about your significant other, offer support and provide positive criticism. While no criticism is easy to accept, positive criticism at least focuses on building a person's spirit. Capitalize on their good qualities while addressing negative qualities. It is easier for others to respond to your desires or wishes when they are not placed in a defensive mode.

It is irrational to expect that you can change another person. Change is a personal phenomenon and occurs when individuals are ready to change. Learn to listen to your significant other, be patient and let him or her know that you believe in them. In your quest to give and receive unconditional love, become skilled at accepting your significant other for who he or she is. God did not create perfect people; therefore you, like others, have both good and bad qualities. It's part of being imperfect human beings! Accept your significant other as is and witness the power of giving and receiving unconditional love.

Expect to Have a Successful Marriage

Expect to succeed in your marriage and be prepared for adversity. Marital distress can wear you down and cause you to feel helpless and hopeless. It seems like the more you try to be positive, the more things get worse, and giving up seems like the rational thing to do. Frustration and disappointment occur in every marriage, but they do not always indicate that the marriage is in serious trouble or must end. However, if you dwell on the negative aspects of your marriage, it will likely lead to the development of a failure mentality. Your mind is powerful and it sets the stage for your performance. If you expect your marriage to fail, you interact with your significant other with uneasiness, low motivation and doubt. Such emotions hinder your ability to bond with your significant other and are highly associated with failed marriage. On the other hand, if you expect your marriage to succeed, you interact with your significant other with confidence, enthusiasm and certainty. These emotions are uplifting and are more often apparent in successful marriage. Shifting your expectations from a failure mentality can lay the foundation for a promising marriage. Positive thoughts lead to positive behaviors, thus increasing the chances of success. Life offers no guarantees, but I can guarantee you that if you expect to fail, you probably will. If you fail, your marriage fails.

Believe that your marriage can be successful and do not dread adversity. Adversity builds resiliency, and resiliency is a precursor to success. Success can be defined either by the process or outcome. It is important to learn the difference. Sometimes you will go through things in your marriage in order to mature and grow. Although you do not desire to experience difficult times in your marriage, the experiences can be considered useful if you learn from them.

Adversity builds resiliency, and resiliency is a precursor to success.

It is irrational to expect that you can give and receive unconditional love in a marriage that you do not believe will succeed. You are capable of having a successful marriage if you decide you want to make it work. Individuals who possess high levels of commitment and dedication often succeed in their endeavors. How committed and dedicated are you to making your marriage succeed? What obstacles are you willing to overcome to succeed in your marriage? Do not base the success of your marriage on where it is today. Look at what it took to get to this point. If you look closely enough you might find that your marriage has lasted as long as it has because you wanted it to. As long as you have it in your heart to succeed, your marriage can withstand the test of time. Giving and receiving unconditional love will become second nature. However, if your marriage is in trouble, ask for help. "Ask and you shall receive, seek and you will find; knock and the door will be opened to you; for everyone who asks will receive, and anyone who seeks will find, and the door will be opened to those who knock" (Mathew 7:7-8). If you desire to succeed, turn to the One who can truly help you. Your desire to succeed in your marriage is achievable if you seek help!

Expect to Change

You cannot expect to give or receive unconditional love in your marriage unless you are willing to change. The change that I am speaking of does not mean that you must give up who you are. Change requires one to be flexible in his or her thinking and doing. Doing the same thing over and over and expecting a different outcome is irrational. If you are experiencing conflict in your marriage, develop a plan to conquer it. The problems you encounter in your marriage are partially your fault. It takes two to quarrel. Some of you walk around daily with a chip on your shoulder. You are mad at your significant other and treat him or her unkindly, but expect him or her to treat you with compassion. Does this make sense? Also, you expect your significant other to be sensitive to your needs and desires, but you fail to respond sensitively to theirs. This self-centeredness is the basis for conflict in most marriage. Search to find out what you can do differently or change about yourself to give and receive the unconditional love you desire.

Change requires one to be flexible in his or her thinking and doing. Doing the same thing over and over and expecting a different outcome is irrational.

It is irrational to expect that you can enter into a marriage and remain the same. You cannot hold on to childhood teachings and previous marriage experiences, especially if they are not productive for you now. The combining of two lifestyles will bring forth change even if you do not want it. You cannot exist in a relationship and continue to think and act as if you are single. Changing yourself can prove to be beneficial to your well-being and your marriage.

Expect to Learn

Lack of knowledge destroys marriages. How do you expect to improve your marriage if you lack knowledge? How often do you equip yourself with information that will help you solve or cope with hardships in your marriage? Your experience alone is not always the most effective way of learning. Vernon Law, a famous baseball player, once stated that, "Experience is a hard teacher because she gives the test first and the lesson afterwards." Instead of engaging in making the same mistakes, try equipping yourself with proper information before the test.

If you desire to give and receive unconditional love, seek counseling and support if you are not successful. Develop a road map for enhancing your knowledge of yourself and your significant other. Learn to validate how your significant other feels, communicate effectively and resolve conflict appropriately. Trying to navigate through your marriage without proper directions or a map can lead to disaster. Matthew 15:14 says, "If the blind lead the blind, both shall fall in the ditch." How can you give and receive unconditional love when you do not know how? Empower yourself by acquiring knowledge and applying it. Lack of knowledge and irrational expectations are the root causes of most failed marriages.

It is irrational to expect that you can give and receive unconditional love in your marriage without equipping yourself with proper knowledge. You should consistently try to learn as much as you can about your significant other and about healthy marriages. This means that you will utilize all available resources. Your willingness to grow and learn will ensure that your marriage will flourish and an abundance of unconditional love will follow.

Expect to Be Generous

Selfishness has no place in marriage. Devotion to yourself will eventually cause you to be by yourself. Showing generosity to your significant other means that you are willing to share your heart and time. Sharing your heart requires you to express emotions. One of the biggest challenges for couples who have become complacent is their inability to share emotions. "You know how I feel, why do I have to tell you?" is commonly stated. This kind of thinking is counterproductive. Guarded or restricted emotional expression cause the most arguments in marriages. Emotional intimacy can only develop in relationships when two hearts are joined. Sharing your heart requires you to express how you feel and not make assumptions. Emotions drive behavior so it is important to learn to understand and share your emotions in a positive manner. Lack of emotional capability, not lack of intellectual capability, is the cause of conflict in marriage. Generosity reduces tension and can potentially influence your significant other to demonstrate the same behavior.

Devotion to yourself will eventually cause you to be by yourself!

Without a doubt, no marriage can grow if individuals do not make time to talk and comfort each other. Telling your significant other that you love him or her is not enough. Most individuals believe what they see, not what they hear. As the saying goes, "Action speaks louder than words." If you truly care about your partner, you will make time to learn about and discuss his or her desires, challenges, joys and concerns. Healthy individuals make time for people and things that are of value to them.

It is irrational to expect that you can give and receive unconditional love without being generous in your marriage. If you struggle to be generous toward your significant other, seek help. Giving of your heart and time is necessary to sustain an emotionally healthy marriage. Never miss an opportunity to express what's in your heart. Furthermore, do not think that money can replace quality time in a marriage. You can replace money, but time is irreplaceable. If you find that generosity is not part of your marriage, then you should strive to develop it. Generosity can be taxing at times, but the reward is life-changing.

Expect to Compromise and Sacrifice

Do you know the difference between compromise and sacrifice? Compromise requires you to meet your significant other in the middle. This approach is widely accepted and practiced in marriages because it positions each person to "win." Sacrifice requires you to give up something for the sole benefit of your significant other. This approach is not widely accepted or practiced because it positions only one person to "win." Societal norms have contributed to the belief that women should be more willing to sacrifice than men. This unfortunate perception has caused tension in many marriages. We are no longer living in the 19th century. I would urge you to practice compromise and sacrifice if you desire to give and receive unconditional love.

At times in your marriage it will be most appropriate to compromise, and at other times it will be most appropriate to sacrifice. If your significant other compromises or sacrifices, recognize and praise his or her effort. This is critical because recognition and praise contribute to gratifying feelings that lead to repeated behavior.

It is irrational to expect that you can give and receive unconditional love in your marriage if you are not willing to compromise and sacrifice. Giving of oneself and feeling good is not gender driven. Everyone desires to be recognized for his or her effort. Recognize that compromise and sacrifice is warranted in every marriage. Life events do not always transpire in perfect harmony. Therefore, you must be willing to compromise and sacrifice as well as honor your significant other for doing the same.

Expect to Be Vulnerable

Do you expect to be vulnerable in your marriage? This is a difficult question to answer because most people associate pain and heartache with being vulnerable, and no one desires to be hurt. Many people view vulnerability as being defenseless. In general, vulnerability is perceived to be very negative. It leads to overwhelming feelings of fear in most people. For this reason, being vulnerable does not sound appealing because the risk is significant. However, you must realize that fear is a reality of life and must be conquered. "For God hath not given us the spirit of fear; but of power, and of love, and of a sound mind" (2 Timothy 1:7). Marriage is risky, but you can have a satisfying experience if you plan accordingly and give unconditional love. People let their guards down and are more willing to face their fears when they feel comfortable. Loving your significant other unconditionally will enhance his or her confidence in the marriage. Only then will being vulnerable not seem so frightening.

It is irrational to expect that you can give and receive unconditional love in your marriage without being vulnerable. To truly experience unconditional love, you must allow yourself to be vulnerable. Guarded hearts do not grow. In my opinion, allowing yourself to be vulnerable is a mark of true love. There is nothing wrong with being vulnerable. Everyone hurts and is weak at some point in his or her life. Pretending to be strong all the time is not healthy and will eventually cause you more hardship in the long run. Learn to express the wide range of emotions God has given you.

7

Strategy #3:

Maintain a Positive Attitude

"Remove Negativity from Your Mind and Heart"

Maintaining a positive attitude is the third strategy to being able to give and receive unconditional love in your marriage. Your way of thinking affects every phase of your life, including your marriage. During my life, I have experienced many things and have been in and out of all kinds of relationships. Through those relationships, I have learned that there are two kinds of people: negative thinkers and positive thinkers. Positive thinkers often search for the good in their significant other and marriage. They are caring, confident, and respectful of others, as well as themselves. They have a strong desire to remove negativity from their mind, heart and marriage. Negative thinkers, on the other hand, often search for the bad in their significant other and marriage. They are insensitive, unsure, and disrespectful. They seem to delight in drama and are unable to remove negativity from their mind, heart and marriage.

My life experiences have taught me that I cannot always control what happens to me, but I can control my attitude. It is easy to be negative when you are hurting, discouraged, and angry. Your inner critic makes it easy to criticize yourself, as well as others, especially when your desires or expectations are not met. It is only natural to want to attack those who hurt you, devalue you, belittle you, or contribute to your suffering. However, fighting fire with fire has never proven to be effective. Negativity begets negativity.

Positive thinkers often search for the good in their significant other and marriage.

As human beings, we are an adaptable species who have the capacity to physically or mentally will ourselves to cope with situations that create distress or conflict for us. When placed in situations that make us feel uncomfortable or threaten our psychological well-being, we search for ways to cope. If we are not capable of escaping distress by physical means, we attempt to change our attitudes. If inconsistencies exist between our attitudes and those of others, we experience conflict. In order to reduce this conflict we change our attitude to achieve a state of psychological balance. This explains the "negativity begets negativity" theory. Let me explain further.

If you are a positive person, but your significant other constantly presents a negative attitude day after day, you will eventually adopt the attitude of your significant other in order to reduce your emotional conflict. Extended and prolonged exposure to unpleasant stimuli causes individuals to adjust to their situation or environment in order to have psychological balance. It sounds irrational to think that someone will become negative to have peace, right? In an attempt to achieve and maintain a state of psychological balance, individuals will adopt the attitudes and behaviors of others. Given this, it important to watch the company you keep and monitor your attitude.

The attitude and behavior you exhibit daily will affect your marriage. Therefore, it is imperative that you remove negativity from your mind and heart. Look to explore and change negative attitudes and thoughts. What kind of thinker are you?

The key to giving and receiving unconditional love begins with your attitude. Dr. David Burns, MD proposed the theory of cognitive distortion. Cognitive distortions are inaccurate perceptions or thoughts that maintain negative thinking and emotions. Let's review some cognitive distortions that lead to negative attitudes. Among these distortions are:

Always/Never Thinking

You think something that has happened will "always" reoccur, or you will "never" secure what you desire or want. For example, if your significant other fails to remember a special occasion, you might think, "He/she always forgets about me and I never get what I want." This thought is negative and can cause you to hold a grudge and feel unappreciated.

It's Never My Fault/Blaming

You blame your significant other for hardships in your marriage and see yourself as a victim. You do not accept responsibility for your actions, emotions, or behaviors because you feel that others caused them. For example, "I would have never hit you if you did not make me angry," or, "I withdraw my love because I have been hurt before, so it is not my fault that you do not feel loved. I do the best I can."

Blame-thinking prevents you from giving and receiving unconditional love because you blame others for your actions and emotions. Another example of this is: "I can't love you the way I want to because my parents never showed me how to love." This kind of thinking restricts you from exercising your personal sense of power. Taking responsibility for your behavior empowers you to change it.

Mental Filter

You select a single negative experience and dwell on it exclusively until your view of reality is clouded. For example, your significant other purchases nice things for your birthday each year, but forgot one year. Instead of being happy and praising your spouse for all the times he or she remembered, you dwell on the one time he or she forgot, telling yourself that your significant other is insensitive. You have a tendency to filter out positive experiences.

Disqualifying the Positive

You dismiss positive experiences by insisting they do not count or matter. For example, your significant other does everything that he or she can possibly do to make you happy because they love you. But, because you do not feel lovable, you reject or minimize his or her efforts. This thinking allows you to maintain a negative belief that is contradicted by your everyday experiences.

Jumping to Conclusions

You randomly jump to a negative conclusion that is not justified by the facts of the situation. "Mind Reading" and "Fortune Teller" are two examples of this kind of thinking.

- **Mind Reading:** you conclude that someone is reacting negatively to you, without checking the facts. "I know he or she does not like me. We have never talked and he or she does not speak to me."

- **Fortune Teller:** you anticipate that things will turn out poorly and you are convinced that your prediction is an established fact. "Why should I try to date him or her? The marriage will not work anyway. It's a waste of my time."

Emotional Reasoning

You assume that your negative emotions automatically reflect the way things really are. "I feel it, therefore it must be true. I feel unlovable, therefore I must be unlovable." This kind of thinking restricts your ability to give and receive love because your feelings do not always reflect reality.

Labeling and Mislabeling

Instead of describing your mistake or inappropriate behavior, you attach a negative label to yourself—as in, "I'm a bad spouse." When someone else's behavior rubs you the wrong way, you attach a negative label to him or her. "He or she's a bad person." Mislabeling is when you describe an event with language that is highly distorted and emotionally loaded. For example: "I'm a failure," instead of, "I made a mistake."

Personalization

You see yourself as the cause of some negative external event which, in fact, you were not primarily responsible for. This distortion is the primary cause of guilt feelings. For example, "It's my fault that my significant other committed adultery. I did whatever I could to please him or her; it's my fault that I did not do enough and he turned to someone else. I should have done more to prevent it from happening."

Are you guilty of using any of the cognitive distortions previously mentioned? You are responsible for your attitude. Your view about giving and receiving unconditional love depends upon what you tell yourself, how you treat yourself, and how you understand your world.

It is important to pay attention to your attitude, especially negative attitudes that affect your marriage, work, and life in general. Recognizing and modifying negative attitudes early is the most effective way to reduce their impact. If you fail to address negative attitudes early, you begin to believe them and inappropriate behavior will follow. While it is normal to protect yourself from being hurt, it is unhealthy to maintain negative attitudes. Unfortunately, most of you struggle to remove negative attitudes because they are deeply rooted in your belief systems. Sometimes you are unaware that you are being negative. For this reason, it is important to check your attitude before you respond to a situation or person. By now you might be asking, "What does my attitude have to do with giving and receiving unconditional love?" I am glad you asked.

Negative attitudes can lead to distrust and apathy. Distrusting others often makes you feel like you cannot give love, which can lead to emotional and physical isolation. Apathy can cause you to have little compassion for yourself or others, which can also lead to emotional and physical isolation. You may find yourself questioning your spouse's intentions and behavior without valid justification. You may unconsciously distance yourself emotionally and overreact to small challenges. You may engage in sex, but detach emotionally to prevent yourself from being hurt. You may stay in a marriage that is not healthy for you. You may engage in activities that undermine your values. Unless you check and adjust your attitude, negativity will become self-defeating and self-inhibiting. Here are two examples:

Case Example #1

John is a 40-year-married, active duty military member, with two children. He is seeking treatment because he is feeling depressed due to marital conflict. Here's his story:

"My wife and I have been married for 12 years and are starting to drift apart. She constantly accuses me of not showing affection. I do not have time to come home and address her emotional needs every day. I take care of all the financial issues and make sure that she has everything she needs. **I want to save my marriage, but I do not have time to be bothered with her pettiness.** I am starting to think that she does not care about my career. I told her that I was a career person when we got married. She recently told me that she did not care about my career and that I should spend more time with her. I do not know what to tell her because I have made too much progress to play around with my career. I love her and my kids, but right now I am focused on what is best for me. She will understand in the long run."

Case Example #2

Michelle is a 28-year-old married female, with two children. She is seeking treatment because she is having a hard time bonding with her husband. Here's her story:

"I don't know where to begin. I just do not connect with my husband. He cheated on me twice and I do not respect or trust him anymore. He apologized and I decided to remain married, but I do not trust him. I am afraid of being hurt. I have tried to let my guard down, but it does not work. In anticipation of getting hurt, I usually do something to upset my husband. I would make him upset to see what he would do. **I know I play games, but I don't want to get hurt**

anymore. Sometimes I care and sometimes I do not. I love him, but I constantly find ways to create drama in our marriage. Life is about protecting yourself because no one else will. I don't want to be hurt again, but I do want to save my marriage."

Maintain a Positive Attitude

Unfortunately, as a result of experiencing some conflict in your marriage, some of you find it difficult to maintain a positive attitude. The inner negative critic tells you to give up on marriage and love. The internal anguish and frustration caused by this thinking makes you behave in a negative way that distances others, thus reinforcing your desire to distance yourself.

Women and men who go through life with negative attitudes are at a greater risk of not giving or receiving unconditional love. Learn to replace negative attitudes with positive attitudes:

Negative Attitudes:

- Rude
- Ungrateful
- Judgmental
- Insensitive
- Unsure
- Pessimistic
- Narrow-minded

Positive Attitudes:

- Peaceful
- Polite

- Thankful
- Non-judgmental
- Compassionate
- Confident
- Optimistic
- Open-minded
- Self-controlled

Maintaining a positive attitude is achievable and can help you give and receive unconditional love. To successfully maintain a positive attitude, you must adjust your thinking. Effectively applying the seven strategies below will enable you to have a marriage filled with joy and bliss.

1.) **Identify distortions** in your thinking. Faulty thinking is unhealthy for you. Identifying negative attitudes is the first step to maintaining a positive attitude.

2.) **Counter your inner critic** by challenging the negative inner voice that attacks and judges you and others. Frequent monitoring of your inner critic prevents distortions from manifesting.

3.) **Identify your strengths** and establish an accurate list of them as well as your resources. Review your list daily to remind yourself of your strengths.

4.) **Use thought stopping.** When the inner critic attacks aggressively, stop the negative thinking and revisit healthy thoughts.

5.) **Accept yourself and others without passing judgment.** Deal with facts only and eliminate negative emotions.

6.)   **Avoid being passive and inflexible.** Express your emotions assertively and be open to feedback and change.

7.)   **Reinforce healthy self-talk.** Use positive affirmations to reinforce healthy self-talk. Examples: "I will have a healthy marriage filled with unconditional love," and "I will not give up until I achieve the result I desire."

Maintaining and fostering a positive attitude requires you to be flexible in your thinking. It is important to understand alternative viewpoints. It is also important to understand yourself. You are your worst critic. What you feel or tell yourself is not always true or accurate. Looking for the good in yourself and others should become a habit, a habit being a point where desire, knowledge, and skill meet. Take time to learn about your significant other by being active, looking for common ground, not assuming differences in meaning, and looking for and respecting individuality. Be mindful that maintaining a positive attitude toward yourself and your significant other does not guarantee that you will receive unconditional love. However, it will allow you to give it. Hopefully what goes around comes back around. Change your attitude and increase your chance of giving and receiving unconditional love. Remove negativity from your mind and heart. Do not allow a negative attitude to rob you of the unconditional love you deserve!

8

Strategy #4:

Love Without Limits

"Don't Be Afraid to Give Your All"

L oving without limits is the fourth strategy to giving and receiving unconditional love in your marriage . Unconditional love sees no limits, feels no limits and believes no limits. Your heart can and will go wherever you direct it. Direct your heart toward God and reap the benefits of loving without limits. Do you know what it means to love someone without limits?

People go through life feeling deprived of love because they are improperly equipped. Many people are conditioned to believe that love can be earned by doing good deed, that we should only love those who love us and that love does not hurt.

Your ability to love yourself and others unconditionally is challenging, because you do not know what true love is. You often look for love in the wrong places. The heart of God and the gospel of Christ is love. Love is compassion, grace, sacrifice, and mercy. Yes, compassion, sacrifice, and mercy! Sometimes you have to be willing to give up someone or something you love to demonstrate compassion for others. God sacrificed His only begotten Son to show us how much He loves us. He continues to show love for you despite your wrongdoing. Loving others, like God loves you, can be difficult, but giving and receiving unconditional love is impossible until you learn to love as He loves. It is easy to fall victim to loving others based on conditions. However, I am delighted that God does not love us based on conditions because we have all fallen short of His glory.

We are cohorts on our journey to reach heaven. Our greatest challenge is loving ourselves and others unconditionally. How can we overcome this challenge? The first step is to love without forcing our rules, requirements, and conditions on others. Let me explain! God loves us so much that He allows us to do as we please. He does not force His love on us or remove it based on our actions. It is true that He has rules for His children and expects us to follow them. But He loves us without limits. He permits us to make mistakes and continues to love us even if He does not approve of our behavior. His compassion for us is immeasurable. He is merciful to those who wrong Him or disobey Him. He does not force us to change. Instead, He provides a firsthand lesson on how to love unconditionally. He teaches us how to love daily and never forsakes us. His love is love without limits. Do you know what this means?

To love unconditionally, you must allow others to exercise their *free will*. Yes! It is your responsibility to hold your significant other accountable, and yes, it is your responsibility to assertively confront him or her when you feel wronged. But remember, you cannot control other people. Understanding the difference between control and influence will enable you to love unconditionally. **Control** means to master or command. **Influence** is the act or power of producing an effect without obvious application of force or direct exercise of command. As mentioned earlier, God does not force us to love Him, and He does not withhold His love. At this point, you are probably wondering how this applies to you and your marriage.

Love to influence, not to control.

One of the major problems that exist in many marriages is withholding love to control others. You have made it known to your wife, husband or significant other that if he or she behaves in a certain way, you will withdraw your love. Is this behavior godly? God commands us to love others without limiting their ability or freedom to exercise their *free will*. I realize that this is a difficult task, especially if you have failed to stand up for yourself previously and have been hurt. As a responsible and mature individual, you decide how to interact with others, but keep in mind that aggressive and controlling behavior does not facilitate openness and growth. If you are upset or desire certain behavior, provide your significant other with as much information as possible to make good decisions, but do not force your thoughts or solutions on him or her. Your job is to influence his or her behavior and let him or her know that you will love them unconditionally regardless of what they decide. This is what God does. He is always present and loves you when you are sick or healthy, happy or sad, obedient or disobedient. He loves us enough to give us total freedom. He wants us to love Him by choice, not by force. When you love someone unconditionally, and they know it, all doubt, fear, and anxiety is removed from their heart. I strongly encourage you to apply this principle in your marriage. Love to influence, not to control.

God instructs us to love others despite their behavior, appearance or flaws. Inflicting pain, and holding grudges or hatred against your significant other will never free you to love without limits. Loving unconditionally is God's remedy to nurturing broken hearts and unhealthy marriages. At times you might question your ability to love those who hurt or upset you, but once you let go, all the harsh emotions and turmoil will disappear. Would you like to experience love like this? Do you believe it is humanly possible to love unconditionally?

I hope you answered, "Yes!" God created you in His likeness and blessed you with the gift of love. All you must do is apply what is in your heart. Do you believe this? Let's explore four strategies you can implement to practice loving others as well as yourself unconditionally.

1. Love like God
2. Understand Love
3. Have Compassion
4. Be Forgiving

Strategy 1: Love like God

God's love is total, says his apostle Paul. It reaches every corner of our experience. It is wide. It covers the breadth of our own experience and reaches out to the whole world. God's love is long - it continues the length of our lives. It is high - it rises to the heights of our celebration and elation. His love is deep – it reaches to the depth of discouragement, despair, and even death (Ephesians 3:17-19).

Strategy 2: Understand Love

Love is not hateful; Love is not resentful; Love is not conditional; Love is not pride; Love is not limited; Love is not a gift from man; Love is not to be taken for granted; Love is not restricted to a specific race or gender. Let me be clear, God is Love.

Strategy 3: Have Compassion for Others

Do you know the difference between sympathy and compassion? Sympathy means to feel sorry for someone, but it does not require you to do anything. Compassion, on the other hand, means to feel sympathetic to another's pain, but it requires action. An individual who is compassionate takes action to relieve others of their suffering. A compassionate person does what is right even in difficult times. When no one else will step up, a compassionate person does. This is what Jesus did for us. A compassionate person does not judge others; instead, he or she helps when warranted. To have a relationship with Jesus and live a Christ-like lifestyle, you must have compassion for others. Compassion fulfills the law of Christ (Galatians 6:2).

Strategy 4: Be Forgiving

Forgiving others is not easy, but God requires you to. If you desire forgiveness, you must be willing to forgive. Refusing to forgive others is a sign of selfishness. God is not selfish, so He expects you to forgive others.

I know it feels unfair to forgive individuals who have emotionally, physically or sexually abused you, neglected you, embarrassed you or belittled you, but forgiveness will enable you to heal. Letting go of anger and hatred is healthy for you and uplifts God's kingdom. Forgiveness is our godly obligation. Also, forgiveness empowers you to take control over your emotions. As long as you harbor unforgiveness, you are empowering those who hurt you. When you release bitterness, you allow God's forgiveness to pour into your life.

Keep in mind that unforgiveness is a negative emotion that handicaps you. If you walk around holding grudges, you will deprive yourself of God's blessings. Some people will offend you—go home and do not think twice about their behavior. You must let go and move on. Remember that no one is perfect, including you. Each one of us has offended someone, so it is important to forgive others so God can forgive you. Pray for those who hurt you because they are hurting themselves. If it is possible and safe, seek to understand their rage; otherwise, remove yourself from the situation and pray for them.

Do not permit anyone to strip you of your gift of love. God created you out of love so that you can love yourself and others. Don't be afraid to love yourself and others unconditionally. The benefits will be great depending on your attitude. Nelson Mandela glorified the importance of loving yourself and living without fear by stating, "As we let our light shine, we unconsciously give other people permission to do the same. As we're liberated from our own fear, our presence automatically liberates others."

PART THREE

HOW TO MAKE YOUR MARRIAGE LAST FOREVER

9

REMAIN One in Marriage

Seek Marital and Spiritual Guidance

"What therefore God has joined together, let no man separate" (Mark 10:9). When we stood before God, family and friends at the altar we became one flesh. We happily stated our vows and promised to love each other forever as one. Unfortunately, because we are not perfect and allow our flesh to consume us, we must remain mindful of temptation and all the negative forces working against our marriage. We must equip ourselves with good relationship skills and spiritual wisdom that is needed to address and resolve our shortcomings both individually and in marriage.

How many couples do you know or have met who seem to be grounded spiritually, but appear to lack effective communication and interpersonal skills? Conversely, how many couples do you know or have met who seem to have effective communication and interpersonal skills, but lack spiritual maturity?

I work with, fellowship with and interact with hundreds of couples who fall into either category daily, and I have learned that they are not capable of giving or receiving unconditional love in their marriages because they are not "one." Some of them are skilled in applying basic psychology and self-help techniques, but lack spiritual maturity. Others are skilled in applying scripture and Christian principles, but lack day-to-day self-help and interpersonal skills. To remain "one" in marriage, couples must be equipped with practical and spiritual knowledge and apply both in their daily interactions. They must live a balanced lifestyle. However, remaining as one is not an easy task because individuals who seek marital counseling are sometimes perceived to be "crazy" or "unstable." Such negative stereotypes reinforce couples' resistance to seeking help, even when they need it.

> *To remain "one" in marriage, couples must be equipped with practical and spiritual knowledge and apply both in their daily interactions.*

In my early years as a therapist, I did not understand why individuals were willing to seek therapy to save marriages that appeared to be destructive and unhealthy. Like others, I did not understand the point. However, after years of listening to hundreds of couples, I began to understand what it means to fight for something you want. While others may view therapy seekers negatively, I view them as role models. They recognize that their marriages are in trouble and seek help. This behavior is far from "crazy." In actuality, individuals who realize that their marriages are troubled, but continue to do the same thing daily without seeking help, might better fit the definition of "crazy."

I have found that individuals who combine professional counseling and spiritual guidance are more capable of developing healthy coping skills, and thus, are more likely to approach marriage conflict with balanced perspectives. Through a combination of marital and spiritual guidance, individuals can acquire knowledge that will enhance their ability to give and receive unconditional love in their marriages. Let's review a session I had with a client who was spiritually grounded, but continued to experience difficulty in her marriage:

Me: How are things going between you and your husband?

Jane: We continue to argue over simple things and end up frustrating each other. We pray for each other and together. We have talked to the pastor several times and received some helpful guidance. Things get better for a while, but we continue to communicate ineffectively.

Me: What contributes to or causes conflict, in your opinion?

Jane: I believe we have different communication styles. Growing up I was told that God would fulfill all my needs. I embraced my spiritual guidance and attempted to apply what I learned daily. My parents did not verbally express their emotions openly and when they had disagreements they prayed and moved on. Occasionally I would hear both of them blaming each other for conflicts that aroused. Neither of my parents took responsibility for their contribution to the conflict. Conversations typically started off with, "You made me." This pattern of communication was common in my household. My parents did not appear to communicate very well, but remained committed to each other through their spiritual maturity. They definitely loved each other, but could not communicate without arguing. I believe I adopted my parents' style of communication. I have a tendency to blame my husband for how I feel. My husband, on the other hand, does not express his feelings. He rarely gets upset, but when he does, he blames me for making him feel that way. We start conversations similar to the way my parents start: "You made me." I respect my husband as the Bible instructs me to, but I am starting to lose respect for him. I pray and ask forgiveness when I am angry and bitter, but I don't know if I love him. I do not understand how a relationship that is filled with so much spirituality continues to decline. If it was not for my faith, I would have probably left by now.

Me: So it sounds like you both attack and accuse each other for feeling a certain way, and this causes communication to come to a halt. Instead of listening, both of you are defending why you feel the way you do.

Jane: You are correct! How can we communicate more effectively? I want to save my marriage and stop fighting so much.

Me: Try using "I" messages. "I" messages are used to avoid blaming others for how you feel. "I" messages facilitate healthy communication by encouraging each of you to take responsibility for your emotions. Instead of saying, "You made me mad because you did not do what you said you would do," say, "I feel mad because you did not do what you said you would do."

Jane: What is the difference?

Me: First, whenever you start a conversation with "you," an individual's natural response is to defend themselves. This decreases the likelihood that they will comprehend anything that is being said to them. As you are talking to them, they are thinking about their defensive response ("I did not make you mad because"). Placing blame on others causes individuals to become defensive. Second, no one can make you feel anything that you do not want to feel. You are responsible for your emotions and have the power to control them. Do you understand why it is important to use "I" messages?

Jane: Yes! I wish I had learned this skill sooner. I definitely know the importance of treating others as I would like to be treated. My spirituality helps me in so many ways, but I often feel that I lack the skills to deal with my marriage on a daily basis. However, the application of this simple communication technique will make a world of difference in my marriage.

Acquiring knowledge through marital guidance and combining it with spiritual guidance will position you to become the whole person that God wants you to be. You must learn how to navigate in the world without being part of it. Every person you encounter will not be spiritually savvy or have excellent inter-personal or communication skills, so it is important to live a balanced life.

I believe in the importance of seeking marital guidance to learn effective coping skills and receive spiritual guidance. This will, in turn, help you learn and understand what God instructs you to do to sustain unconditional love in your marriage. Think of marital guidance as the mechanism that provides the coping skills you need to apply the knowledge you learn through spiritual guidance. Marriages are difficult to sustain without God's presence and without effective interpersonal and communication skills.

Until you learn to achieve balance, you will continue to experience unnecessary hardships in your marriage. You will not always understand everything that happens in your marriage. However, even if, at times, you struggle to sustain it, the **Word** teaches you to: "Trust in the LORD with all thine heart; and lean not unto thine own understanding. In all thy ways acknowledge Him, and He shall direct thy paths" (Proverbs 3:5-6). Work to nurture your spirituality, but remember to develop effective coping skills along the way.

People navigate through life and relationships by using their "common sense" instead of developing effective coping skills. In my opinion, the sole use of common sense is not very effective because "common sense" is really not so common. Individuals typically do what is common to them. For example, as a young boy I treated girls disrespectfully because I observed that behavior daily. I knew my behavior was wrong, but behaved that way because it was "common" to me—i.e. everybody else did it. Individual life experiences develop "common sense," so be mindful of others' experiences before you make assumptions that they are using this so-called "common sense." No two people are the same. With this in mind, do not solely rely on what is common to you, especially if it is not working. Seek guidance.

To sustain unconditional love in your marriage, start by restoring or enhancing your spiritual relationship with God. Through God all things are possible. As you connect with God, you become free from the shackles of anger, frustration and resentment. This does not mean that you will not continue to experience difficulty, as others are liberated to use their *free will* as they see fit. However, it does mean that you will be better equipped to cope with this. If you are spiritually grounded, but continue to have difficulty sustaining unconditional love in your marriage, seek marital guidance. As stated earlier, relationships require work. Therefore, after you pray, attend church and consult with your pastor, and be prepared to learn and apply effective communication, stress and anger management skills that you can use daily to sustain unconditional love. If you maximize your options, I guarantee that sustaining unconditional love will come with minimum distress. You should always strive to enhance your spiritual, emotional, intellectual and physical well-being. This is how you will successfully remain one in marriage.

10

Practice Loving Self Unconditionally

"Love from within illuminates outwardly."

The most effective method for giving and receiving unconditional love and making your marriage last forever is to practice unconditional love for yourself Unconditional love begins and ends with you, not your spouse. When you love yourself, you make it easier for your spouse to do the same. I realize that the ability to love yourself unconditionally can be difficult at times, especially if you have experienced hardships such as sexual, physical or emotional abuse. However, remember that your life experiences do not define who you are. Unfortunately, bad things happen to good people. Your ability to cope with hardships defines your true character. Do not fall victim to loving yourself based on conditions. Love yourself regardless of your appearance, background, or economic, social or financial status. I understand that this is a complex task because people can be very judgmental. Remember that God did not create perfect spouses or people. Some individuals may appear to have it all together. They might even appear to be perfect, but Jesus was the only perfect human that ever walked this earth. Do not live your life stressing over being perfect. Instead, live it doing the best you can. Challenge yourself to objectively eliminate emotions, expectations and attitudes that make you feel unlovable.

You are special because you share the image of God. When you are feeling down, remember that life is a gift from God. Need I say more? Your ability to love yourself unconditionally depends on what you tell yourself, how you treat yourself, and how you interpret your world. If loving yourself requires your spouse to approve of you, you might find yourself occasionally feeling frustrated, helpless and powerless. Seeking the approval of others can cause low self-esteem and contribute to demoralizing behavior. Work at loving yourself and improving your self-esteem. People with high self-esteem view themselves positively. They often feel good about themselves and appreciate their own worth.

Now that I have your undivided attention and you are inspired to love yourself unconditionally, let's look at empowering self-love techniques that you can implement to improve your self-esteem, helping you learn to love yourself unconditionally.

1. Love God first
2. Set your own personal standards
3. Use encouraging, positive language
4. Identify your strengths
5. Eliminate self-defeating/irrational thinking
6. Do away with perfectionist thinking

Self-Love Technique 1: Love God first

God created you to love Him, but many of you look for love in all the wrong places. True happiness and unconditional love for yourself and others will not occur until you learn to love God first. God is love and He loves you unconditionally. You are His child. Do not distance yourself from your Father when evil things happen to you or your loved ones. Remember that God gave us all the gift of *free will*. Be mindful that your attempt to walk righteously does not exclude you from experiencing bad things. Others have *free will* too, and when they choose to be of the world instead of God, evil things will happen. Evil is present where God is absent. Keep God in your heart, mind and soul, and loving yourself unconditionally will come easily. Unconditional love for self and others is only possible if you reorder your love and put God first.

Therefore if any man be in Christ, he is a new creature: old things are passed away; behold, all things are become new (II Corinthians 5:17).
But seek ye first the kingdom of God, and his righteousness; and all these things shall be added unto you (Matthew 6:33)

Self-Love Technique 2: Set your own personal standards

To start loving yourself, simply set your own standards. Do not live your life according to how others view you. Avoid comparing yourself to others and using belittling words such as stupid, unattractive, powerless, worthless, and shallow to describe yourself. Pay close attention to how you define and describe yourself. Stop negative self-attacks.

Self-Love Technique 3: Use encouraging, positive language

"The tongue of the wise useth knowledge aright: but the mouth of fools poureth out foolishness" (Proverbs 15:2). When you talk to yourself and to others about yourself, use positive and inspiring statements. Such statements are called affirmations. Effective use of affirmations can help you change problem areas in your life. Identify a problem in your life and set a goal. Use affirmations that describe that goal. Some examples of affirmations include:

- I am lovable and worthy of being happy in my life and in my marriage.
- I am intelligent and feel really good about it.
- I can cope with life challenges in a healthy manner.
- I handle disappointment calmly and reasonably.
- I have a right to make mistakes.
- I can let go of my need to control others.
- I cope with despair and pain rationally.

Learn to write affirmations that use present tense, define what you want, what already exists, and what makes you feel good. Use specific, personal, action-oriented words that are short and to the point. Develop a list of affirmations that are meaningful to you and speak them daily. If your affirmations do not produce your desired outcome, write new ones. Remember that what you say to yourself and to others about yourself is often stored subconsciously in your mind and in theirs.

Self-Love Technique 4: Identify your strengths

Conduct an accurate and honest self-assessment. Develop a valid list of your strengths and assets. If you suffer from low self-esteem, it probably did not develop overnight. Remind yourself of your strengths daily and take an inventory. Use the inventory to help you identify blessings, accomplishments and goals you have achieved that support your dreams and ambitions.

Self-Love Technique 5: Eliminate self-defeating, irrational beliefs

Question your old beliefs and replace them with new ones. Too often you hold on to the unhealthy beliefs with which you grew up. Some of your beliefs are healthy and some are not. If the following beliefs are in your mind, eliminate them:

- If I ask for help, I'll look weak.
- If people knew the real me, they would dislike me.
- If I fail, I'm a loser.
- I should never feel hopeless, helpless, powerless, tired or depressed.
- I am nothing unless I am loved.
- I should be totally self-sufficient and independent.
- I have to be right all the time or I won't be respected.
- I am the only one who understands me and who can solve my problems.
- If I try hard enough, I can succeed at anything and everything
- Some people are better than others.
- I need to be smart, rich, powerful and attractive to be happy.
- Life isn't fair, and I can't handle it.
- It reflects poorly on me if my marriage does not work.

Eliminating self-defeating, irrational thinking can help you see and experience life more objectively. Your mind is powerful, and, if used inappropriately, it can cause you to self-destruct. Examine your beliefs and ask yourself several questions. What evidence do I have to support my beliefs? Are my beliefs beneficial or healthy? Do they make me feel good or bad? After carefully reviewing your beliefs, you might find that you need to eliminate some of them and replace them with new ones. Don't be discouraged or beat yourself up during this process. Changing your way of thinking can be a complex process. After all, you did not become the person you are in an instant.

Self-Love Technique 6: Do away with perfectionist thinking

While it is important to look, feel and do well, remember that you are not and will never be perfect. Striving for perfection can lead to unrealistic expectations for yourself and others. Do your best to accept yourself while enhancing your performance and having fun. Life is too short to live it thinking you must do everything perfectly or not at all. Perfectionist thinking can lead to hard work and no pleasure. You cannot do it all. Enjoy life, yourself and your spouse, and ask for help when you need it.

Improving your self-esteem and loving yourself unconditionally can be one of the most rewarding things you will ever do. Do not let others rob you of your gift of life. God created you out of love so you can love yourself and others. Don't be afraid to love yourself. The benefits can be profound.

To love yourself unconditionally, practice the self-love techniques listed above daily. Additionally, share your commitment with your spouse and use the quote below for inspiration.

"The ultimate lesson all of us have to learn is unconditional love, which includes not only others but ourselves as well."

—*Elisabeth Kubler-Ross*

11

Assess Your Level of Marital Intimacy and REBUILD

Strategies for saving marriages and developing healthy connections tend to focus almost exclusively on encouraging individuals to practice effective communication skills. While effective communication is very important, assessing and understanding the different levels of intimacy is just as important to making your marriage last forever. Understanding the three levels of intimacy is not the sole solution for saving or enhancing your marriage, but it may help you gain insight into some of your more difficult and underlying challenges. This chapter places emphasis on the importance of exploring and understanding the three levels of intimacy.

Three Levels of Intimacy

Physical intimacy – is best defined as the physical display of affectionate or sexual energy that stems from one's desire to be comforted or stimulated through touch. Physical intimacy is easier to develop in relationships than emotional or spiritual intimacy because it is evolves from behavioral attributes (hugging, kissing, touching, sex, etc.) that provide immediate gratification and/or satisfaction. It is common for individuals to settle for physical intimacy, especially if they do not know how to give or receive emotional or spiritual intimacy.

Emotional Intimacy – involves self-disclosure of one's personal experiences, emotions and thoughts. The desire to give and receive love and comfort from your spouse leads to the development of emotional intimacy. However, trust must be present for emotional intimacy to flourish. While emotional intimacy is critical to establishing and sustaining healthy marriages, it is not as important as spiritual intimacy.

Spiritual Intimacy – evolves as a result of two people coming together and connecting based on common faith and purpose. They strive to be equally yoked in most facets of life, including their spiritual walks, professional and personal development and commitment to creating harmony in their relationships. A couple involved in spiritual intimacy find purpose and meaning in their co-existence and achieve marital harmony as a result of sharing similar ethical foundations and worldviews. They pray for each and other and their relationship. They put God at the center of their relationship so that no one person is above the other.

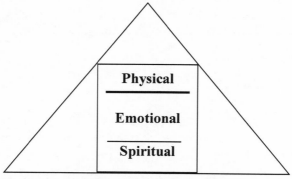

The Three Levels of Intimacy pyramid diagram depicts what is most important starting at the bottom to what is least important at the top.

The lowest level of the pyramid represents what is most important in making marriage last forever. While physical intimacy is important in relationships, no relationship can be sustained for extended periods without some level of emotional harmony and spiritual connectivity.

Some couples struggle to sustain harmony and connectivity in their marriages because they may have developed good physical chemistry, but lack spiritual connectivity. In my professional experience, I have learned and observed that marriages built on physical foundations are ten times more likely to collapse than those built on spiritual foundations. Physical intimacy may build relationships, but spiritual intimacy will make them last forever.

If you learn nothing else from this chapter, please be mindful that spiritual and emotional intimacy can intensify physical intimacy, but physical intimacy cannot intense spiritual or emotional intimacy. Once spiritual intimacy has been established, you will have greater success at establishing intimacy on the emotional and physical level.

> *Spiritual and emotional intimacy can intensify physical intimacy, but physical intimacy cannot intensify spiritual or emotional intimacy.*

According to social scientists, 40 to 50 percent of all marriages in the United States will end in divorce or permanent separation. The divorce risk is 60 percent for individuals who are working on their second marriage.

In my professional experience, I have learned that some individuals who struggle to make their marriage last forever and are at higher risk for divorce because they do not understand the risk factors associated with marital discord. The challenge of building and sustaining a healthy marriage is not an easy task and couples who have built relationships based on the wrong level of intimacy are at a greater risk of divorce.

Assessing your level of intimacy and understanding which one your marriage was built on is the first step toward making it last forever. As they say, knowing is half the battle.

Use the Marriage Intimacy Assessment below to begin the assessment and rebuilding process.

Marriage Intimacy Assessment (MIA)

The purpose of this assessment is to provide you with a good sense of the level of intimacy in your marriage, and thus, to assess what your marriage was built on.

Read each statement and circle T for "true" or F for "false." Please be honest as you answer the questions:

Physical Intimacy

1. I married my spouse because I was physically attracted to him or   her **T F**
2. I would not have married my spouse if I was not physically attracted to him or her **T F**
3. Sexual energy is vital to sustaining a healthy marriage **TF**
4. Physical intimacy is easier to develop than emotional **T F**
5. My marriage was built on physical intimacy **T F**
6. It is okay to remain in a marriage that is primarily physical in nature **T F**
7. I had to learn to love my spouse after the decline of physical attraction **T F**
8. I struggle with expressing my emotions so I use physical intimacy to express my needs and desires **T F**

9. I enjoy kissing, touching and sex more than I enjoy disclosing feelings and emotions **T F**
10. I have always thrived in relationships that were more physical in nature **T F**

Give yourself 1 point for each "True" answer.
Total: _____

Emotional Intimacy

1. I married my spouse because we have great emotional synergy and connectivity **T F**
2. I married my spouse because I felt and still feel very comfortable disclosing my personal thoughts and feelings **T F**
3. I trust that my spouse will always do right by me and strive to understand my feelings **T F**
4. I openly express how I feel and feel validated most of the time by my spouse **T F**
5. Giving and receiving affection is very important to my spouse and me **T F**
6. My spouse is very good about comforting me when I am in distress **T F**
7. Crying and sensitivity are acceptable in my marriage **T F**
8. I never feel emotionally neglected **T F**
10. I have always thrived in relationships that were more emotional in nature **T F**

Give yourself 1 point for each "True" answer.
Total: _____

Spiritual Intimacy

1. I married my spouse because we have mutual faith and confidence in each other **T F**
2. My spouse and I share a common purpose and our marriage thrives as a result **T F**
3. My spouse and I believe in being equally yoked and striving to do so in our marriage **T F**
4. My spouse and I value and respect each other's purpose **T F**
5. My spouse and I are and have always been committed to creating harmony in our marriage **T F**
6. We have found purpose and meaning in our co-existence **T F**
7. Praying together and for each other is commonplace **T F**
8. God is at the center of our relationship **T F**
9. My spouse and I share similar ethical foundations and worldviews **T F**
10. I have always thrived in relationships that were more spiritual in nature **T F**

Give yourself 1 point for each "True" answer.
Total: _____

Scoring: Compare scores for each section above. The section with the highest score reflects the level of intimacy that your marriage was built on. If your marriage was not built on spiritual intimacy, do not panic. This means that you should begin the rebuilding process in order to make your marriage last forever.

Rebuild

Here are 10 strategies for rebuilding:

1) Commit to the rebuilding process
2) Focus on healing from marital distress
3) Identify strengths and challenges in achieving the proper level of intimacy
4) Define what you would like to see in your marriage
5) Have a transparent conversation about the level of intimacy in your marriage
6) Honor each other
7) Build shared meaning and purpose together
8) Seek professional and spiritual guidance
9) Pray together and for each other
10) Let Go and Let God

Be mindful that the quality of your marriage is not determined by what you go through, but how you get through it. Create safe conditions in your marriage and it will thrive.

12

ASK DR. BUCKINGHAM

ANSWERS to QUESTIONS from MARRIED COUPLES in DISTRESS

As a guest writer and marriage coach for *Black and Married with Kids*, the web's most popular destination for guidance on African American marriage and parenting, I receive hundreds of questions via email on a weekly basis from couples who are experiencing marital distress. I find pleasure in responding to the anonymous emails because I believe that marriage is worth fighting for. With this in mind, I try my best to provide the best advice possible as a marriage coach. I praise these individuals for seeking guidance.

If you are experiencing marital distress, I hope that you find my responses beneficial.

Marital Distress:

I have been married for six years to a man I feel like I just don't love and am not sure if I ever did. I was going through a phase in which I wanted to get my life right with God when

I met my husband in church. He said all the right things and I married him after seven months of knowing him. We have such a personality difference and I just don't look at him as the man I love. However, we do have a 3-year-old son to raise so I am torn between staying in a loveless marriage, or risk disrupting my child's family life. My husband and I do not connect mentally, physically or sexually. We have tried and I just don't feel a connection with him. We are currently in counseling but I feel like we are prolonging the inevitable (divorce). As soon as we try to communicate it escalates to an argument quickly and then we are both frustrated. He says he loves me but I just have don't have emotions towards him. I feel stuck.

Question:

Can I Thrive in a Loveless Marriage?

Answer:

Sorry to hear about your marital discord. Unfortunately, I do not have enough information to truly understand the severity of your situation. However, I have worked with many couples who have different personalities and struggle to connect mentally, physically and sexually. Some struggle in the beginning of their marriage and others struggle as they move forward. From my professional experience, I have learned that many couples are unhappy because they believe that love is the key to sustaining a long-term marriage. This distorted belief about love is the leading cause of divorce. The truth is this: the exhilarating feeling of being in love typically lasts eighteen months to two years, a time period in which most marriage experts refer to as the "honeymoon stage." During this timeframe, individuals go out of their way to please each other. They take action and strive to be optimistic. Love drives this behavior, but does not sustain it.

Marriages do not endure because of love, but because of the work that is invested to develop and nurture love. The ability to give and receive love requires action. Thriving in a loveless marriage is not easy, but can be accomplished if you are willing to take action. Please consider the four strategies listed below:

1. Explore What Love Means to You. What is love? Understanding love is the key to receiving and giving love. Love is an emotion that is influenced by action. Love is not hate; love is not resentment; *love is not conditional*; love is not pride; love is not limited; love is not to be taken for granted; love is God. God created people to be unique and provided instruction on how to embrace and work through those differences. Loving like God can help provide clarity. Spiritual intimacy will always outlast emotional, physical or sexual intimacy. Also, educating yourself about various love styles can prove to be helpful. In my book, **Unconditional Love: How to Give and Receive Unconditional Love in Your Marriage,** I provide an overview of love and unconditional love as well as identify different love styles.

2. Explore Why You Married Your Husband. This is critical because he presented some qualities that were good enough to convince you to say, "I do." Conduct an accurate and honest assessment of your marriage. Develop a list of strengths daily and take an inventory. Use the inventory to help you identify blessings, accomplishments, and goals that you have achieved in your marriage. Try developing compassion for your husband. A compassionate person does not judge others; instead, he or she helps when warranted. To have a relationship with Jesus and live a Christ-like lifestyle, you must have compassion for others. Compassion fulfills the law of Christ (Galatians 6:2).

3. Eliminate Self-Defeating and Negative Thinking. You stated that you are currently in counseling, but do not feel hopeful. This negative thinking does not lead to positive resolution. You get out of therapy and your marriage what you put into them. You have the power to change what you do not like. The self-fulfilling prophecy is real. You must be mindful of the perceptions you develop about your husband and marriage. There is a difference between being realistic and being negative. Reality means that we face our challenges head on and accept them for what they are. Negativity, on the other hand, means that we look for and focus on the bad in situations. You can be realistic without being negative. Hope for the best and be prepared for the worst. Love is a matter of the heart, but how we decide to love is a matter of the mind.

4. Understand That Differences Are Not Always Bad. I have found that individuals express love differently because they come from different backgrounds. Understanding how individuals feel loved and how they express love is critical to the bonding process. The *Five Love Languages* by Gary Chapman is a great book that provides insight into the importance of seeking an understanding of others' love language in order to bond with them based on their specific needs and desires.

Please consider applying the four strategies outlined above and remember that the easiest way to find and sustain love in your marriage is to let God guide you. If He orders your steps, you will be blessed with a wealth of love. Considering that you met your husband in church, I assume that he possesses some of the Godly qualities that you desire in a man. If he is willing to work on his shortcomings and strives to love, give your marriage a chance. Falling in love happens when sexual and emotional chemistry is present, but sustaining love happens when God is present. Remaining in a marriage without feeling love can be difficult and heartbreaking, but you can turn it around and thrive. Love is fluid, but commitment is not.

Marital Distress:

My husband and I have been married for almost three years; we were together off and on for almost 10 years before that. My husband and I separated once before because of his lack of ability to provide and lead our family. After about a year apart, he seemed to have gotten himself together and came back. Satisfied with the change I saw in him, I agreed to marry him.

Old habits die hard, it seems. I am a very driven and accomplished woman. I strive to make good decisions that will benefit our family; I work hard to make sure our family lives a good life. My husband, on the other hand, is back to his lazy, selfish ways. He makes decisions based on what's best for him without thought to the future and best interest of our family. Despite my arguments to wait until we were stable financially, he decided to have knee surgery (which could have waited at least 6-7 months). He has not worked in over seven months and currently has no income.

We are in dire financial straits. I can't respect him as a man, much less my spouse. His laziness angers me to the point where I can't stand to look at him, much less treat him as head of the household. We've tried counseling at my urging to no avail. I understand that a woman is supposed to follow her husband and speak life into him, but how can I follow a parked car? More importantly, how do I know when it's time to cut my losses and move on without dead weight?

Question:

What Should I Do If My Spouse is Not Contributing?

Answer:

Unfortunately, you have learned that there is nothing that you can do to get your husband to work unless he wants to. Talking, nagging or arguing is not going to change or motivate him. As you stated, "old habits die hard." The best indicator of an individual's future behavior is his or her past behavior. Change is sustained only when individuals truly embrace it and see the value in it. Be mindful that values influence behavior and some people value working and some do not. This is tough because financial distress is among the top contributors to marital discord.

In regards to your questions, let me offer a few thoughts that might help you cope with your marital distress.

Thought #1: You cannot follow a parked car. It appears that your husband lacks an understanding of what it means to be the head of the household and the importance of working. His inability or refusal to work threatens the family, your marriage and his walk with God. God himself worked and expects us to work. According to Genesis 2:15, He placed Adam and Eve in the garden to "tend and keep" it. He created man and woman to rule over creation. This requires work. Work is honorable and demonstrates faith in God. Your husband may require some mentoring. Encourage him to speak with a pastor, a life coach or a professional counselor. He might also benefit from reading my book, **A Black Man's Worth: Conqueror and Head of Household.** Chronological age and desire do not make a man, a man. He might need someone besides you to help him learn the importance of fulfilling his role as the head of the household. He might need a tune-up in order to get moving and to function like he previously did.

Thought #2: Most people would agree that your husband should contribute to your family as the head of the household. He is required to lead and set the tempo in the house. However, this does not mean that he has to work outside the home and make a lot of money. I have worked with couples who have non-traditional roles regarding who works outside the home. They do not focus on who is making the money as long as both are contributing to the family. One spouse takes care of the children at home while the other spouse goes to work. This may or may not work for your marriage. This kind of thinking is called a reframe. Sometimes we have to alter our thinking and be flexible in our roles in order to make our marriage work.

Thought #3: Assertively express your concern about finances and let him know that you will make some changes if he does not contribute. Discuss job opportunities, the economy, and his concerns or motives for not working. Set deadlines and give him time to step-up. Monitor his behavior and see if he is actively trying to secure a job. Cheer for him instead of nagging or arguing with him. Positive energy motivates people, not negative energy. Also, make sure that you conduct yourself in accordance with God's guidance.

Try to exhaust all of your options before calling it quits. Do right by your spouse and remember that life is not fair, but God is. If you honestly feel that you have done your part as a loving spouse and an obedient child of God, then cut your losses and move on.

Marital Distress:

I have been married for seven years to a wonderful woman and we have four children. One child is in college, one in high school and the youngest children are 5- and 4-years-old. I never was good at talking much and always kept things inside. I know my wife loves me, but I don't think that she is in love with me anymore.

We had a good marriage, but I let myself go because I was not happy personally. I gained about 60 pounds after saying I do and about 22 months ago I lost my mother, who was the love of my life. Unfortunately, my wife and I were not in a good place at the time of my mother's death. If we had sex once a month it was a good month. I reached out to an old friend for support and we started texting each other, which led to me talking about what I wanted to do to her.

My wife saw the text messages and hit the ceiling. It took some time, but we kind of patched things up and tried to move forward. We even started seeing a Christian Counselor. Then, on Thanksgiving, my wife asked to use my notebook and found telephone numbers of pay-for-service women. I told my wife that I had never done anything with anyone besides her, but she told me that she wanted to move out. She tells me often that she doesn't know if I am the one anymore.

Over the past 6 months I have been sleeping in the basement. I love my wife, but it seems as though she does not want to be married anymore. She is not willing to work on our marriage at this point. Although we both still say that we love each other, my wife tells me that she sees me as a friend. Unfortunately, I lost my father about two months ago and my wife was very supportive while I was grieving.

Question:

I Messed up, but How Can I Get My Wife Back?

Answer:

I am sorry to hear about your troubled marriage and the loss of both of your parents. Unfortunately, you have experienced a great deal of adversity in a short time span. I pray for your strength and commend you for seeking guidance. My initial response to your question is as follows: work on you. I highly recommend that you seek professional counseling for individual purposes. You mentioned that you are not good at expressing yourself and have struggled with managing your weight and finding personal happiness. A professional counselor can help you learn effective communication skills, assist you in finding a happy place, and guide you in restoring trust in yourself and your marriage.

You will continue to struggle in your marriage until you resolve your personal challenges. Learning how to communicate effectively and acquiring knowledge about techniques that can help restore trust in your marriage will serve to be very beneficial. Remember that no marriage can survive without effective communication and trust. Your wife's trust in you is shattered. By sending inappropriate text messages and storing the contact information of call girls, you have allowed mistrust to enter into your marriage. This is unfortunate because trust is the foundation of any marriage and when it disappears, insecurity, paranoia, anger and fear become commonplace. When the latter things are present in a marriage, intimacy and love will take a hit.

Listed below are five strategies that might help you restore trust in your marriage and get your wife back:

1. **Be truthful moving forward and take responsibility for your actions.** Lying about the simplest thing can create additional suspicion and set you back significantly. No matter how you feel, it is important to communicate in an open and honest manner. Mean what you say and follow through with action. Lying is not an option.

2. **Commit to change.** Be willing to do whatever it takes to modify the behavior that created the mistrust. If you have been devoted to yourself, change immediately. Remember that devotion to yourself will cause you to be by yourself.

3. **Share openly.** Give your wife access to your cell phone, social media accounts and email contacts. This might be difficult to do, but if you desire to restore trust and save your marriage, do not allow your self-righteous need for privacy to override your need for love. This is a short-term sacrifice for a long-term benefit. Privacy is important, but so is trust.

4. **Re-examine your values and personal needs.** If you value marriage, then spend more time learning how to make it work. Be aware of and work through selfish and self-centered thinking. If you find

yourself focusing on your personal needs without considering others, you are in a bad place. Some people love the idea of marriage, but not the personal and interpersonal work that comes with it.

5. **Eliminate fear of living without your wife.** Fear of living without someone is not a good reason to stay in a marriage. True happiness occurs when you enjoy living with them. Allow love to guide your actions and fear.

By applying the five strategies listed above, you will be better positioned to regain the trust of your wife. However, be mindful that it will take time for your wife to trust again. It appears that her emotional wounds are deep. If you want to get your wife back, get help and make some lifestyle changes. Develop habits that will nurture your marriage and allow it to grow. Think positive, remain calm and be honest as you move forward on your journey toward marital restoration.

Marital Distress:

I've been married almost two years come May. My husband and I have been butting heads for a while now. I found out five months after we were married that he was entertaining text messages from his ex-girlfriend. It started right after we were married with a "congratulations" on Facebook and progressed into sexting. I found out because he slipped and hit his face on the concrete and the hospital called me and gave me all his belongings. The girl texted him while I had his phone. I was heartbroken to see that he would destroy our trust and marriage. It seems as though so many other issues have surfaced now that I know who he actually is.

I'm at my breaking point because we don't know how to communicate. We continue to have yelling matches or we shut down. What should I do?

Question:

My Husband Is Sexting with an Ex: What Should I Do?

Answer:

I am sorry to hear about your marital conflict. I am going to start off by encouraging you to be mindful of whom you receive advice from. Some people might advise you to leave your husband instead of seeking help. Many would argue that you should take care of yourself and cut your ties from a man who is unfaithful and unworthy. Others might argue that seeking guidance or counseling is not going to help. I encourage you to check your source before taking action. In today's society, it is easy for people to take the past of least resistance, especially when we have been victimized. What do I mean by taking the path of least resistance?

Taking the path of least resistance means that we will take the easiest way to reach our goals and solve problems, especially when in distress. For example, walking away from our marriage is often perceived to be much easier than learning to forgive and restore trust. I realize that some marriages cannot be saved, but I also believe that some marriages can be saved if both parties put in work instead of taking the path of least resistance. Unfortunately, a large percentage of people walk away from their marriage when faced with adversity because leaving appears to be the easiest and best solution at the time.

Whatever you decide to do to resolve your marital discord, make it a personal journey first by spending more time with yourself. Think about what you need and want in order to remain married. Remember that self-love is the best love because you can show your husband what you desire and need. Work to relieve your heartache and establish a loving relationship with yourself. I assure you that you will feel more equipped to make a decision that is best for you and your marriage.

Considering that you have remained with your husband after finding out about the sexting, I assume that you would like to save your marriage. If this is accurate, I highly recommend that you seek counseling. I realize that you are devastated, but I assure you that learning how to process and communicate how you feel is the key to reducing your distress and restoring trust in your marriage. If you have a desire to save your marriage, you and your husband must learn how to engage in open, honest and respectful communication. Therefore, individual and marital therapy should not be optional, but necessary.

Yes, you have been victimized, but you do not have to act like a victim. Hold your husband accountable, take care of yourself and remember that your fate is partially determined by your work. Please consider contacting me for coaching.

Marital Distress:

I am married with two children: a girl and a boy who have Autism. My husband and I have been married for 4 1/2 years. We are not as connected as we used to be. There are a lot of things that I could name that he is not doing for my sake or his kids' sake; mind you they are 3-, and 5-years-old.

I am drained in the marriage and am not getting what I need from it.

Question:

When Is It Time to Leave My Marriage?

Answer:

I am sorry to hear about your unhappiness in your marriage. However, in providing marital therapy over the past 17 years, I have never advised anyone to walk away from their marriage. I am pro marriage, but I am also pro health. What does this mean?

I believe that every marriage is worth fighting for and can be salvaged if two people are willing to work and develop healthy coping skills. In my coaching and therapy sessions, I simply help people understand what is healthy and unhealthy. A healthy marriage is comprised of two individuals who care and love enough to listen, assist and express compassion toward each other on a regular basis, especially during times of distress.

If you are not getting your needs met in your marriage, I recommend that you take a look at yourself first. This is important because you need to examine how you express your need for affection and help. It is not uncommon for individuals to become verbally abusive and short-tempered when they are unhappy, overwhelmed and burned out. After looking at yourself, I recommend that you ask your spouse to attend professional counseling if you can afford it. By attending counseling you can gain insight into how to improve your marriage. Walking away from a marriage should only happen, in my personal opinion, when an individual refuses to help him or herself. You cannot force anyone to be happy or healthy.

It appears that you have invested a great deal of love, time and energy into your children and husband, but now it is time to take care of yourself. Never make long-term and potentially devastating life or marital decisions when in distress. Deciding to leave or to stay in your marriage will become clearer as you become healthier.

Marital Distress:

I've been married to my husband for three years. We've been together for five years. My husband has struggled with drugs and alcohol for 22 years. I fell hard for his charismatic ways, but during our marriage, he has cheated, used drugs, drank and is verbally abusive. He drinks on the job. He drinks and drives. He has no moral compass. I tried counseling and meeting with our pastor but he refuses to change. I am at a loss. What are my options? Are there any groups or someone that can help me to strengthen myself so that I can walk away?

Question:

How Can I Develop the Strength to Walk Away from My Alcoholic Spouse?

Answer:

If you have not already learned about co-dependency and how one becomes co-dependent, I recommend that you attend Al-Anon family group meetings. Group meetings can help you learn about co-dependency and how others have effectively dealt with their addicted loved ones. You will receive emotional support and learn to recognize the pathologies in your marriage.

Unfortunately, many spouses of addicts believe that they can fix or resolve their partner's drinking and/or drug addiction. While this thinking provides hope, is positive and noteworthy, it is inaccurate. From many years of working with addicts, I have learned that a larger percentage of them typically do not get better or remain sober unless they are personally invested in the treatment and recovery process. Al-Anon can help you gain insight into this unfortunate trend and strengthen you as you strive to emotionally withdraw from your husband.

If you are interested in receiving individual coaching to become stronger, please visit my website (www.drbuckingham) and schedule a free 20-minute consultation assessment. I can teach you how to develop positive and healthy coping skills that will enable you to be happy without depending on your husband.

Dealing with addiction can be very challenging, intense and confusing at times. Given this, I commend you for seeking assistance. After attending Al-Anon group meetings and receiving individual coaching, you will be better equipped to live the happy life that you desire and deserve.

Marital Distress:

I have recognized that my wife has past issues that I now have to deal with. They include being cheated on in a four-year marriage, being molested by her stepdad (he went to jail and her mother didn't take her or her sister to court to testify; they let him out and he came right back into the house as the man of the house), her real father was a true player and she has sisters that are also her cousins. She says she has dealt with her issues internally and doesn't feel like those affect our marriage. But I see them in all situations, arguments, and other instances between us. It is now to the point where I don't even want to be around her. I love her but I am having a really hard time trying to find a reason to stay in this marriage. With all that being said, how do I continue on in this marriage while being the scapegoat for those issues?

Question:

How Do I Remain in a Marriage with My Emotionally Damaged Wife?

Answer:

I am very familiar with your story, especially from a professional perspective. As a psychotherapist, I have provided therapy to thousands of couples who have similar marital challenges. Through my work I have learned that unresolved childhood trauma can definitely create disharmony in marriage. I conducted a research study that explored how Black women's childhood experiences impacted their perceptions and abilities to achieve marital satisfaction.

My research showed that 100 percent of the women modeled behavior that they observed or witnessed in childhood. With this in mind, it is important to understand that we are all by-products of our environments. This does not mean that we cannot change or overcome our childhood hardships.

Remaining in a marriage with an emotionally damaged woman is not easy, but there is hope! First, you should recommend that your wife attend individual therapy. Your wife might have some underlying issues associated with trusting men. Considering that you are a man, she might be projecting her issues onto you. This is common behavior for women who have been betrayed by men. Also your wife might be suffering from Post-Traumatic Stress Disorder (PTSD). PTSD is a psychological disorder that is present when individuals experience significant difficulty in moving forward after experiencing significant childhood or adult trauma. Being molested and experiencing cheating can be very traumatic. A professional counselor can assess whether or not your wife suffers from PTSD.

Second, you should consider marital therapy. It is important that you gain insight into your wife's challenges and let her know that you are committed to helping her work through her challenges. You can also benefit from sharing your emotions and thoughts.

You stated that you love your wife, but you are finding it difficult to find a reason to remain married. Here is one reason: you promised before God to support your wife through sickness. Most people do not view psychological illness as sickness, but it is. You made a covenant so you should focus on making your marriage your number one priority. Pray for your wife's healing and get her the help that she needs.

I do not believe that you have to remain in a marriage with an emotionally damaged woman if your wife is not willing to get help. Her problem is your problem and your problem is her problem. This is what oneness means. Your current marital woes do not necessarily reflect your future. Be and encourage the change you would like to see in your wife and marriage. She needs your empathy, guidance and support now more than ever before.

Marital Distress:

I have been married for five months, however, my husband and I have been together for almost 10 years. We have a 2-year-old daughter and we have lived together for almost four years. We have had many ups and downs over the years, most recently on Valentine's Day.

My husband was off from work that day but he did not tell me. Instead, he decided to go out of town to visit a close relative of his. I found out he was not at work that day because I had called his job and they told me his department did not work that day. So I checked his bank account and saw recent purchases in the city he was visiting that were nowhere near his job site. So I proceeded to call him and ask what time he got off work (not making him aware that I knew he wasn't there.) He responded saying he had just gotten off and was in a store looking for something to buy me on Valentine's Day.

All I could think about is that he was cheating on me. When he got home that night, he was empty-handed and still unaware of what I knew. So I told him that I had called his job and they said he didn't have to work. He tried to cover that saying he had to work in another department. Then I said a friend of mine spotted him in one of the stores where he had made a purchase in so I asked him to tell the truth. He paused then admitted that he was in this particular city and not at work. I asked why he had to lie about it. He responded saying that I would have nagged him if I knew he had the day off and was going out of town. He wanted the day to himself until I got off work.

I asked who was he with all day and he said a close relative who helped him pick out my Valentine's Day gift. However, he came home empty-handed saying stuff was expensive and we were going out the following night. I pointed out to him that he made both of us look like fools. For him to lie about going to work only to go out of town and spend Valentine's Day with his relative and not his wife was disappointing and hurtful. I don't know if I can trust him fully. Although he did state it was the only time he had lied like that and I just so happened to catch him. Not sure how to take the marriage seriously. I want my marriage to work but I don't want to be anyone's fool.

Question:

I Caught My Spouse in a Lie; Should I Think the Worst?

Answer:

In reading your dilemma, I believe that your husband's behavior is an indicator of other potential problems that might exist in your marriage. You mentioned that his reason for lying to you was because he did not want you to nag him about coming along. Based on this statement, I am wondering if he feels smothered at times. Also, I am wondering if he does not feel comfortable discussing certain topics with you. I mention these two things not to blame you for his inappropriate behavior, but to identify topics for discussion.

I agree that your husband's behavior was hurtful, but you must make a decision to forgive him if you desire to create harmony in your marriage. Forgiveness is a prerequisite to restoring trust. Without forgiveness, you will not be able to trust him again. I know that it feels unfair to forgive, but forgiveness will enable you to heal from the emotional pain. As long as you harbor disappointment and pain, you will walk around with a grudge.

I recommend that you have a discussion with your husband about being trustworthy and express your fear of being made to look like a fool. If you struggle with trusting your husband, you will have a hard time sustaining a healthy marriage. In all of my years as a therapist, I have never seen a healthy marriage work or last without trust. Trust sets the stage for love to prosper. Understand that trust must be present and mutually expressed in order to have a healthy marriage.

If you desire to remain married and have a harmonious marriage, I do not recommend that you start to think the worst. Be careful of what you think and look for because you might just find it. Looking for negativity is not healthy for you or your marriage. Trust is a core marriage value that must be present if you want your marriage to last forever. Without trust, there is no respect, and without respect, there is no communication. Please seek professional counseling if you cannot restore trust with your husband.

Marital Distress:

My husband and I have been together for six years and he will be 27 in October (I'm 23). Since April, my husband has been withdrawn and he told me that he was not attracted to me. We have two beautiful children together and I adored my husband. I was there for him while he was in the Army and when he got out. He had never deployed and had a horrible time at our first assigned duty station. He got out of the Army on Feb. 14, 2014. I have never been the type of woman who dressed up. I was more of a tomboy due to molestation that happened to me by two different family members when I was seven and nine. So I felt the need to be invisible and my world was good because he was the one who "saw" me.

Fast forward a couple months and he now tells me he wants to separate. He stopped going places with me and our children, and now completely shuts me out. I went through a stage of begging him, asking how I could fix it. I lost over 20 pounds and fixed the way I dressed. I changed my attitude, to no avail. I was beyond hurt when he automatically refused marriage counseling by my pastor. He then told me he wanted to move out shortly after I discovered pictures of him and other women. Out of hurt, I ran away. I packed up my children and our things and went to my mother's house. The next thing I know, I was paying for utilities for a house I no longer stayed in and paid for his phone bill because I loved him. I wanted to show him that even if he didn't have a job (and had no desire to find one), I would do my best to support him.

I loved this man, but he flaunts his new women by the front door so I can see them and it kills me inside. I feel hurt and betrayed and just flat-out used. I have been nothing but faithful and devoted to him. I am already starting to separate myself from him, but it kills me. What makes a woman good enough for love? How did he stop loving me? Why am I not good enough?

Question:

What Makes a Wife Good Enough for Love?

Answer:

First of all, you are good enough to be loved. As a child of God, you deserve all that your heart desires. Unfortunately, you are looking for love in all the wrong places and for the wrong reasons.

You cannot find and be loved by a man who does not know how to love. Based on your description of your husband's behavior, he does not know what it means to honor and cherish a woman. He appears to be selfish, self-centered and very insensitive. Please be mindful that love does not dwell in these kinds of men. Love can be found in God. Never devote yourself to a man who has not devoted himself to God. When a man learns to love God, he learns what it means to love others, how to sacrifice and work through suffering, and, most importantly, how to honor and respect the women in his life. Please stop searching for love in the wrong places. I am glad to hear that you are starting to separate yourself from him so that you can begin to heal. I empathize with your pain, but I strongly advise you: do not turn back. You deserve better.

Besides looking for love in the wrong place, you are looking for love for the wrong reason. It appears that you are looking for love from a man who will "see" you for you. If you desire to be with a man who will "see" you for you, stop feeling pressured to change yourself. While it is important to look, feel, and do well, remember that you are not and will never be perfect. We were born into sin and all have some demons we must cope with and conquer.

From a spiritual perspective, I believe that a wife is good enough for love because she is God's most valued creation. However, from a secular or practical perspective, I believe that a wife is good enough for love when she learns to love herself. In your case, improving your self-esteem and loving yourself unconditionally can be one of the most rewarding things that you will ever do. When you love yourself, you demonstrate for your husband what it looks like. Do not let your husband rob you of your gift of love. God created you out of love so that you can love yourself and others.

I realize that the ability to love yourself might be challenging, especially since you have experienced hardships in the past such as sexual and emotional abuse. However, remember that your life experiences do not define who you are. Unfortunately, bad things happen to good people. Your ability to cope with hardships defines your true character. Given this, I highly recommend that you seek professional counseling outside of the church. Psychology and theology are not the same. The best approach is to combine both disciplines. Professionals like me have received specialized training and have acquired a wealth of knowledge and experience in dealing with abuse and trauma survivors.

Remember that your worth is not defined by your physical appearance or emotional disposition, but by your god-given attributes. Sometimes we do not always understand our troubles or recognize our blessings. Being separated from your husband is troublesome, but it may also be a blessing. You cannot expect God to protect you from all bad things, but you can rest assured that he loves you. After all, you are a Queen!

To begin the process of acquiring knowledge to help you heal your wounds, please secure a copy of my book: **A Black Woman's Worth: My Queen and Backbone.**

Marital Distress:

My wife and I have known each other for five years before we were married and we've been married for four years. We have three beautiful children and I have one from a separate marriage. Before we were married, I was unfaithful and did some things that I am not proud of to this day. Since our marriage, I have been faithful to her but the past always seems to come back and she always brings it up. I've noticed two years ago the decline in physical intimacy in our marriage. Sex seemed to be more of chore than something she enjoyed. We've gone to therapy together and I've put out all of my shortcomings to her in a safe environment, but still no change in her attitude.

Lately we've become more distant and we've talked about it. She says that she has given up all emotional attachment to me but is trying to get it back. Yet she feels that when I tell her that she is beautiful, I'm only trying to get sex out of her. This is not the case at all. Now I've begun to see she is texting one of her male coworkers more than me and it's making me very nervous that she is cheating, even though when I ask, she says there's nothing going on. She just says she needs to hear from someone else that she is beautiful because she feels ugly and fat. I love my wife but I won't stay with her if we can't move on from the past. At this point I don't know where to go from here. Could you please give me some kind of advice on what I should do?

Question:

Can a Troubled Marriage Survive Without Forgiveness?

Answer:

To begin, I would like to thank you for seeking counsel. Unfortunately, a large percentage of men do not ask for help. Your willingness to fight for your marriage is noteworthy. Also, your willingness to admit your wrongdoing and to attend therapy is noteworthy.

Based on your description of your current marital tension, it appears that your wife never did forgive you. Your wife's lack of interest in physical intimacy is connected to her lack of emotional intimacy. It is probably safe to speculate that she married you with resentment and bitterness in her heart. This is not good. Without forgiveness, a troubled marriage cannot survive. It is impossible to thrive in life or love if one lives with nastiness in his or her heart.

Forgiving others is not easy, but God requires us to forgive. Refusing to forgive others is a sign of selfishness. God is not selfish, so He expects us to forgive others. However, it is not easy to forgive individuals who have emotionally, physically or sexually abused us, neglected us, embarrassed or belittled us, but forgiveness will enable us to heal. Letting go of anger and hatred is healthy and uplifts God's kingdom. Forgiveness is our Godly obligation. Also, forgiveness empowers us to take control over our emotions. As long as we harbor unforgiveness, we are empowering those who hurt us and we remain stuck in the past. When we release bitterness, we allow God's forgiveness to pour into our life and marriage.

I speak about forgiveness from a Godly perspective because forgiveness is a matter of the heart. Keep in mind that unforgiveness is a negative emotion that handicaps us. In order to be released from this bondage, we have to heal our heart. With this in mind, I highly recommend that you and your wife seek spiritual counseling.

I have found that individuals who combine professional counseling and spiritual guidance are more capable of developing healthy coping skills and approaching marriage conflict with balanced perspectives. Through a combination of marital and spiritual guidance, you and your wife can acquire knowledge that will enhance your ability to thrive in your marriage.

Acquiring knowledge through marital guidance and combining it with spiritual guidance will position your wife to become the whole person that God wants her to be. I believe that it is important to seek marital guidance to learn effective coping skills as well as receive spiritual guidance to learn and understand what God instructs you to do to sustain unconditional love in your marriage. Think of marital guidance as the mechanism that provides the coping skills you need to apply the knowledge you learn through spiritual guidance. Marriages are difficult to sustain without God's presence and effective interpersonal and communication skills. If you have concerns about your wife having an emotional affair, assertively express your concerns before your assumptions and worry build up and cause you to act irrationally.

Until you learn to achieve balance in your marriage, you will continue to experience unnecessary hardship. Marriage can be difficult at times and sustaining it can be challenging, but the Word teaches us to: "Trust in the LORD with all thine heart; and lean not unto thine own understanding. In all thy ways acknowledge Him, and He shall direct thy paths" (Proverbs 3:5-6). Strive to connect with your wife spiritually, then emotional and physical intimacy will come. Remember that the heart represents our soul. Work to nurture your spirituality, but remember to develop effective coping skills along the way.

Marital Distress:

I married a spoiled momma's boy. At the time, I didn't know how spoiled he was. His mother helps him financially and he relies on both of us for money.

Question:

How Can I Know If My Husband Married Me for Love, Not Financial Security?

Answer:

Love and financial security are two factors that propel a large percentage of individuals to head to the wedding alter. However, they are also two factors that lead to divorce. Given this, I personally believe that love and money do not mix. Let me explain.

Love is a subjective factor. Love is the feel good part of marriage that causes individuals to share their heart, mind and soul. We were created to love each other and our very existence is rooted in our ability to give and receive love. Love makes us feel connected, important and cared for. It is one of the most powerful emotions that a man or woman can experience in life and love.

Financial security on the other hand, is an objective factor. Financial security is about survival and offers a means to experience life with little to no monetary stress. People rob, kill, lie and cheat to acquire financial security. Some even enter marriage as a means to secure financial stability. Unfortunately, financial security is one of the most influential survival factors that drive individuals' behavior.

While we need love and financial security to survive and to be happy in our marriage, love and money do not mix. As the old saying goes, "Money can't buy you love." Some people believe that love conquers all, and I agree.

Love is emotionally-driven. In contrast, financial security is money-driven. Love requires a good heart, good intentions and the desire to do right by others. God created us out of love so that we can love. On the other hand, financial security requires a good bank account, sound investments and the desire to secure worldly possessions. God wants us to be financially prosperous, but not at the expense of failing to love others. Love and money is only a good mix when love is the main ingredient.

Here are two signs that indicate your marriage is based on financial security, not love.

1. **Money Focused Conversations**. If your significant other spends more time talking about your bank account than he does talking about how he makes your marriage thrive, then your marriage might be based on financial security. If he equates money with love, you are in trouble. The thinking is this: "If you love me, you will buy me this or that!" It is important to discuss money matters, but it is as equally important to discuss love and how to sustain it. Money comes and goes, but love should be forever.

2. **Frequent Arguments About Money and Financial Security.** If your significant other has a sense of entitlement and believes that money is more important than the quality of your marriage, then your marriage might be based on financial security. Pay attention to whether or not your significant other verbally attacks you because you fail to address his need for financial security. Consideration and affection are typically missing in marriages that are primarily driven by money. If the money is not right or tight, there is a fight.

At the root of most marital discord is money. The love of money is what makes marriage fail. Financial security is a blessing that occurs when we do God's will, which is to love others. If your marriage is not filled with love, unwavering companionship and commitment, you married for the wrong reason.

Marital Distress:

My husband and I have been married for three years now but he has been cheating on me even before we got married. When I was pregnant with our daughter, his ex was also pregnant by him as well. Our babies would have been a few weeks apart but she had a miscarriage. After our daughter was born, he promised that he would stop cheating, I forgave him and tried to move on, but not too long after that I found nude pictures of another ex that he was sexting. This is getting to me as the list of women goes on. Every time I try to tell him how I feel hurt, he makes me feel like it's my fault that he cheats. I am holding on because of our daughter and the promise I made to God in my marriage vows. But I am at my breaking point and I can't handle it anymore.

Question:

My Spouse Is a Chronic Cheater; What Should I Do?

Answer:

I am not a big supporter of divorce because I am a Christian who believes in the power of change, maintaining holy vows, and I understand that God hates divorce. However, God does allow divorce in certain circumstances. There are two biblical grounds for divorce. The first is adultery and the second is if a Christian is married to an unbeliever who wants out of the marriage.

Divorce is not good, but neither is emotional abuse, degradation or infidelity. God demands that we respect, cherish and honor our significant others. The seventh commandment states, "You shall not commit adultery" (Exodus 20:14). Adultery is not only a sin against one's mate, but an attack on the sanctity of marriage, and a course of behavior that can cause chaos in the lives of many people. Most importantly, adultery is a sin against God.

Your desire to sustain your marriage because of your daughter and your promise to God is noteworthy, but know that God desires us to live in peace. Coping with infidelity can be very challenging because it threatens our ability to live in harmony. Listed below are three recommendations that can help you make the best decision for all involved.

1. Take Care of Yourself. It is important not to deal with this issue alone. Seek spiritual and professional counseling so that you can develop balanced thinking. Through spiritual counseling you might be encouraged to work hard on forgiveness and sustainability in spite of the emotional abuse. While spiritual counseling provides helpful information from a biblical standpoint, you may not get an objective, balanced view. For this reason, it is important to also seek professional counseling so that you can learn how to cope with psychological issues. Coping with domination, belittling and disrespect can contribute to psychological problems such as post-traumatic stress. Dealing with trauma can cause you to feel like you are walking on eggshells, and you may continue to have emotional and physical reactions when you are reminded of the infidelity. Given this, it is critical to cope with infidelity both spiritually and psychologically.

2. Take Care of Your Daughter. Make sure that your daughter has an outlet to process and express her concerns if she has been exposed to marital distress. Do not try to hide your distress from your child. Let her know that you are working through some things with her father. However, do not share the details of your troubles. Taking care of your child's emotional well-being is good regardless of your decision to remain married or divorce.

3. Ask Your Husband to Get Help. I have counseled hundreds of individuals who suffer from sexual addictions. Reasons for infidelity vary greatly from one individual to the next and seeking help can provide answers. Through my professional experience, I have learned that adultery is a psychological shortcoming that is manifested through inappropriate behavior. I have successfully helped "cheaters" identify psychological issues that contribute to their sexual indiscretions. Your husband might benefit from discussing his behavior with someone besides you. See if he will make a commitment to save your marriage.

I wish you the best and hope that you seek help to cope with your unfaithful mate. Feelings of betrayal, mistrust and confusion do not go away over-night so be patient with the process. Time is your best intervention. Remember that forgiveness empowers you to move on. However, forgiveness alone will not help you move beyond the pain. Take your troubles to God and take care of yourself so that you achieve the best outcome for you. If you do decide to end your marriage, make sure that you have thought about potential challenges and the way ahead.

Marital Distress:

I am a married-late, 30-year-old with two kids by my wife and an older son from a previous marriage. My concern is that, in my opinion, my wife is very insecure because of my outgoing personality and her weight. As a result we do not have sex on a regular basis. I feel she is jealous of my first child's mother and me.

I do not know how to deal with her because she does not communicate, and she internalizes all of her feelings and emotions. I feel that I am only staying in this marriage because of our kids and she knows it.

I am not perfect and I know she has issues with me that I need to work on by myself. Our problem is I own up to my issues and she does not. I have tried upgrading her to hip new things and fashions and she rejects them. She always says that I am looking at other women in her presence.

I know this is wrong and I am not making excuses, but I am not pleased with her personal hygiene and housekeeping at all. She knows it because I complain about it all the time.

Question:

My Wife Is Insecure: What Can I Do to Make Our Marriage Work?

Answer:

I believe that you are on the right path in regards to owning up to your character flaws. Self-awareness and self-accountability are important steps toward resolving marital challenges. However, verbally acknowledging your wrongdoing does not make it right. If you want to truly make a difference in your marriage, you should make sure that your actions speak louder than your words. Bottom line: stop looking at other women. If your wife is not pleasing to your eyes, maybe you need to pay more attention to her heart.

Physical intimacy is important, but marriage is about being connected emotionally and spiritually.

In regards to your wife's insecurity, you cannot make her understand your concerns, however, you can strive to love her unconditionally. If she is not sure or confident of herself, I recommend that you try practicing positive regard. Positive regard is the ability to love and treat someone in a nonjudgmental manner with the hope that they will change internally, not because of you. Complaining and telling someone what you want is not the same as loving them as they are showing them what you want. You mentioned that you tried upgrading her to hip new things and fashions, and she rejects them. Have you tried asking her what makes her happy and comfortable?

You can make your situation better and your marriage work by seeking counseling. Poor communication is not something that you can ignore and expect things to change or improve. Your wife's inability or difficulty with expressing her emotions will continue to cause problems. Your frustration and disappointment in your wife will also continue to cause problems because your behavior will not improve until you improve your thinking. Learning how to communicate and cope more effectively is the key to sustaining a healthy marriage.

Love for your children is not a good reason to stay in an unhealthy marriage. Remaining married because of guilt or fear is not the same as remaining married because of innocence and confidence. Have confidence in your marriage and extend that confidence to your wife. Try listening to her concerns and do not rebut. Her perception is her reality. However, this does not mean that it is correct. It does mean that you will have more success if you listen and allow her to feel however she wants. Your responsibility is to hear her out and to let her know that she is entitled to feel how she likes. Also, let her know that you will only address emotions that are going to propel your marriage to the next level. Remember: you cannot open someone's eyes if they are ok with having them closed. Change is a personal phenomenon. Each individual has to be willing to sacrifice and compromise in order to make the marriage work. Establish a contract with your wife that focuses on generating positive energy, respect and positive regard. You should feel free in your marriage, not imprisoned.

Marital Distress:

I've been married to my husband for a year now but I've been with him for four years and my husband and I have sexual relations maybe once a month. At times we can go for six weeks without any. He is an excellent dad to his children; actually, I feel he loves them more than me. He works; he provides for his family and is a great guy. But when it comes to affection, romance and sex, it's two thumbs down. As his wife, I have listened to every excuse that he has given me as to what could be the problem. I have asked him to seek a doctor to try and get down to the problem. I practically took him to the office; he did a few STD tests and was negative. He never went back to get down to the root of the problem.

I am a Pisces; I am a very affectionate, romantic and sexual person. He knew this when he first met me and not to mention he has a sexy wife. To keep this serious, it just feels like we're roommates. We pay bills, take care of the kids, and we may go out to a movie or dinner. But NO touching or goo goo eyes unless I initiate it. Now, I just feel like the man in this marriage, always being the one to touch him. It makes me feel like it's so one-sided.

Do I think he's cheating? Sometimes I do. The reality is, when he does have the time to be intimate, he uses the "I have to work" excuse. But I have to say he did cheat on me in the past while I was pregnant with our 2-year-old son so I can't put anything past him. I'm so confused at this point because I truly love him and have done a lot for him to help him get back on his feet as well as helped as much as I could with this issue. But this is not normal and has every sign of an unhealthy marriage, and it doesn't look like he's willing to change. I'm the type of woman that doesn't need a man to validate me, so I'm going to put on my running shoes and head for the door.

I really need some advice because I know good men are hard to find so when you have one you should keep him. But if you're unhappy at times because of this situation, just what is a girl to do?

Question:

What Do You Do When There Is No Romance in Your Marriage?

Answer:

Based on the description that you provided regarding your marital discord, I would argue that physical intimacy is problematic in your marriage because there is little spiritual or emotional intimacy. I drew this observation from your statements. You said, "He is an excellent dad to his children, actually I feel he loves them more than me. To keep this serious, it just feels like we're roommates. We pay bills, take care of the kids and we may go out to a movie or dinner."

Believe it or not, some men do not like to engage in physical intimacy if they do not feel connected emotionally or spiritually. This is confusing for most women because some men have had one- night sexual encounters without being emotionally connected. While this is true, there is a difference. Men can have one-night sexual encounters without emotional intimacy because the expectations are different. Marriages that are primarily sexual in nature are often about generating sexual synergy and nothing more. Once the "good" sex is over, so is the marriage.

Your marital discord is rooted in deeper issues. Please understand that spiritual and emotional intimacy is needed in order to have a healthy marriage. Spiritual intimacy sets the foundation for a healthy marriage and emotional intimacy helps build trust. Spiritual intimacy allows individuals to connect on faith and purpose. You should ask your husband the following question, "What is our purpose?" Having a common purpose gives meaning to your marriage. Also, I encourage you to address your trust issues.

It is difficult to have true emotional intimacy without trust. Marriages have a less likely chance of survival if trust is missing. Please address your trust issues with your husband. When trust is present in a marriage, individuals feel comfortable disclosing their personal thoughts and experiences.

To answer your question, What Do You Do When There Is No Romance in Your Marriage?—the answer is simple: seek help. You are focusing a great deal on the lack of sexual and physical intimacy in your marriage. While these things are very important, they cannot sustain a marriage. You should strive to address what I perceive to be spiritual and emotional challenges with your husband. Explore whether he is emotionally or physically challenged in regards to making love.

In working with thousands of men over the years, I have learned that men's decision to withdraw from having sex or expressing intimacy stems from two areas: emotional distress and/or sexual dysfunction. Once you identify your husband's challenge, you will be better equipped to determine if you should remain married. Furthermore, you will learn how to respond to him appropriately.

I do not believe that a wife or husband should walk away from his or her significant other if the person has potential and is willing to grow. However, it is important to be mindful of the fact that a man or woman will not change unless he or she wants to do so. So, do not think that you can change your husband if he does not want or desire help. You can support your husband and ask him to attend professional counseling, but if he refuses, then what? Pray about it and seek God's guidance. If he refuses to seek help, you should still consider it for personal growth. Contact me, if you think you are willing to take that step.

Marital Distress

My husband and I have been married for three years now, but he has been cheating on me, even before we got married. When I was pregnant with our daughter, an ex-girlfriend of his was also pregnant by him too. Our babies would have been a few weeks apart but she had a miscarriage. After our daughter was born, he promised that he would stop cheating and I forgave him and tried to move on. However, not too long after I forgave him, I found nude pictures of another ex that he was sexting.

This is getting to me, as the list of women goes on.

Every time I try to tell him how I feel and how hurt I am, he makes me feel like it is my fault that he cheats. I am holding on because of our daughter and the promise I made to God in my marriage vows. I am at my breaking point and I can't handle it anymore.

Question:

My Husband Has an Adulterous Heart: What Should I Do?

Answer:

First things first! You are not responsible for your husband's adulterous and cheating behavior. The ability to feel and experience love is a gift from God. Furthermore, how we express our love is also a gift from God, and it is called *free will*. No human has the power to control another human. We simply influence behavior, but do not determine it. I want to clear this up because you should not feel guilty because of your husband's sexual indiscretions.

People also wonder if romantic relationships outside of marriage are permissible as long as there is no actual sexual intercourse (sex-texting or lusting after another). The bible teaches us that marriage is an exclusive romantic and sexual relationship between husband and wife. Jesus said: "You have heard that it was said, 'Do not commit adultery.' But I tell you that anyone who looks at a woman lustfully has already committed adultery with her in his heart" (NIV, Matthew 5:27-28).

Many would advise you to leave your husband immediately because they believe that once a cheater, always a cheater. While there is some truth to this saying, I believe that anyone who defers to God will and can be savaged. God will forgive the sin of adultery if the person sincerely repents.

I believe that adulterous behavior is the by-product of a loss of soul. Where there is adultery, there is poor judgment and self-destruction. Proverbs 6:32 tells us that a man who commits adultery lacks judgment and, as a result, will destroy himself. The bible mentions adultery as grounds for divorce (Matthews 5:31-32, 19:9), but there is no requirement to do so.

If you decide to save or reconcile your marriage, I highly recommend that you and your husband seek help. He might have a sexual addiction or he might just be manipulative and self-centered. Either way, he is not going to do right by you without taking responsibility for his behavior. If he refuses to get help, you should consider moving on. Remember that you not only have to respect yourself, but you have to be a role model for your daughter. Respect is not automatic, it is demanded. You cannot expect to be treated special or like a queen, if you allow him to manipulate you and treat you like a second-class citizen. If he cannot do right by you and your daughter as the head of the household, he does not deserve to be in that position.

Marital Distress

I have been married for just a year. We were dating off and on for 10 years because he was deployed a lot and I was stationed elsewhere. We both already each had a son from previous relationships, and three years ago we had a son together. BLENDED! Over the past 7-8 years my husband has gained about 175 pounds and he gets depressed. When I tell him to cut back, he snaps at me. So I fall back and let him do his thing, then he says I am not supportive.

This is my issue with SEX, because all he does is sleep. Before my marriage I had a serious problem with initiating intimacy, and in a sense I still do because I was afraid of rejection or ridicule. But with him sleeping all the time, like right now while I am typing this, he is asleep!

What can I do? It's boring. He's not affectionate; he doesn't just come up and hug me, or kiss me. And he's always home, too... no smacks on the butt...UNLESS...he's feeling some type of way. Other than that, he's not playful, no morning kisses, no goodnight kisses. When I talked to him about it, he said he has never been that affectionate.

I thought maybe it was because of our distance before, but this is a real problem. He is not emotionally available for me. I begged him to please go to counseling and he has refused twice. I don't know anymore. Any advice? Am I asking too much?

Question:

I Want My Husband to Be Emotionally Available: Am I Asking Too Much?

Answer:

No, you are not asking too much. Emotional intimacy is what makes us feel connected and loved.

Ninety percent of the women I see for individual consultation and marital therapy struggle in their marriages because they are married to men who are emotionally unavailable.

Listen to me when I tell you that men who are emotionally

unavailable can and will suck the life out of you and will not experience much distress while doing so. I make it sound as if men are evil and have no heart. This is not the case by far; some men just miss the mark when it comes to recognizing and responding to emotions, especially if they are not truly interested in you or are emotionally unavailable— "Emotions, what are those?"

Some men are emotionally unavailable because they have difficulty recognizing emotions, and others choose to be emotionally unavailable because they are consumed by career aspirations, school or work obligations, peer pressure, success, selfishness, heartache from a previous relationship or unresolved mental health problems.

Men who are emotionally unavailable do not invest heartfelt time and energy into relationships with women. Your chances of being hurt are greater during this period of emotional seclusion.

Emotionally unavailable men want what every man wants— your time, your body, your mind, your companionship and your undivided attention. He wants you to be there for him emotionally, physically and spiritually, but will not give the same in return. Most women do not get or understand this.

If your husband continues to refuse help, I highly recommend that you seek help. This is very important because men who are emotionally unavailable often project their distress onto those close to them. Remember that anyone who struggles to love him or herself, will probably struggle to love others. Also, I recommend that you should seek professional help because you mentioned that your husband gets depressed and you still have a problem with initiating intimacy. By seeking counseling, you can learn how to cope with your husband's depression more effectively as well as work through your fear of rejection.

It is extremely important to take care of yourself emotionally, physically and spiritually so that you can maintain your sanity. If your husband is not willing to do the work, I do not believe that you will get what your heart desires - intimacy. Your husband must understand that it is impossible to love with a purpose, if he does not live with a purpose. With this in mind, I want to remind you that your husband's participation is needed to make your relationship work. Your marriage will not survive if you are doing all the work, and he is not doing any. Once your mind is clear and you are at peace, you will be able to make better decisions regarding the future of your marriage.

Marital Distress:

My husband and I have been together for 10 years and married for five of those years. We've been separated since January. We started having some serious issues about two years after we were married and it just seems that we can't get back on the right track. We're both Christians, and take our faith seriously. That's a major reason we haven't divorced. We have two children together, 7- and 2-year-olds, and he has a 14-year-old son from a previous relationship. The reason for the separation is because of trust issues stemming from drug addiction, finances, emotions and infidelity.

Two years ago he lost his job and I wasn't working because we had just had our second child the previous year. We had to move in with family due to the job loss and I know that really hurt him having to do that. I was disappointed when he lost his job, not because he lost it, but because he wasn't honest with me about the way he lost his job. I had to admit I was embarrassed because of the situation. I pushed through it and I realized everyone falls short but it's okay, no need to be embarrassed, it is what it is. I tried to be supportive and let him know that at least we have family that is able to help us, but I also let him know that not being honest with me is unacceptable.

I landed a job six months later. We were able to get our own place again and start the road back to getting on our feet. He recently got a job, which is great, but for about a year and a half when he was unemployed, he treated me horribly including no sex for 18 months and not offering any emotional support. I realize now that he was treating me like that because of his own issues, but that's no cause to take it out on me. In addition to earlier issues, the relationship during this time was so bad that it led to our separation. The additional issues seemed to be magnified ten times during this time.

I had individual therapy (nine months) and we have talked to a marriage therapist at our church (three sessions). The therapy was very beneficial to me because it helped me realize how I contributed to the issues by not expressing my feelings. I would always put his needs before mine without any concern for having my own needs met; a realization that I have expressed to him. At the same time, I suggested marriage therapy for both of us, with the intention of him realizing how he also contributed to the marriage breakdown, but the therapy was short lived.

Since we have been separated, I don't know if we're going to make it. Just when I get a glimmer of hope for the marriage, he goes right back to putting his needs first without any consideration for how I feel. I have no idea where to go from here. I've been praying everyday about the situation and I'm trying to be patient, but I am ready to move on. I don't like the idea of being separated but I just can't have the stress around me anymore. I refuse to let it affect my happiness and joy, but I have no idea where to go from here.

Question:

Can My Marriage Survive Separation?

Answer:

Sorry to hear about your marital discord. It appears that you have tried several things to save your marriage with little success. I am glad that you attended individual and marital therapy. You gained insight into what you were doing to contribute to the tension in your marriage, and you tried to encourage your husband to gain insight as well.

To answer your question, "Can Marriage Survive Separation?" my response is as follows: It depends. It depends on the purpose of the separation.

If the purpose of the separation is to engage in self-reflection and to do some personal work so that each individual can be rejuvenated, I would say that marriage can survive separation.

Relationships are a composite of two individuals who make a whole. However, sometimes individuals need a break from ongoing marital tension because it can be very difficult to process and to think clearly during the midst of a storm. Separation affords individuals with the ability to reflect on what has happened, which in return can begin the process for reconciliation.

Some people believe that absence makes the heart grow fonder, because we typically desire what we lack. I only partially agree with this statement because it depends on what we are lacking and what we desire. In your situation, absence is not helping because your husband is not displaying the qualities that your desire. Therefore, you are not lacking.

In my professional opinion, I do not believe that long-term separation is good for any relationship because there is no opportunity to work on the challenges. I suggest that you continue to pray and do some additional personal work too. You might have to accept the fact that your husband will probably not change. Some people struggle with replacing selfish behavior with selfless behavior and your husband might be one of them. Remember that true happiness occurs when you enjoy living with someone. Given this, I recommend that you make a list of things that you desire in your marriage and present them to your husband. The list should include solutions. It is easy to be problem-focused, but hard to be solution-focused. However, the latter is your saving grace and can save your marriage. Marriage is about oneness and togetherness. Love is fluid, but commitment is not. If your husband wants to remain married, he will strive to do the work. If he does not attempt to do the work, you might have to seek and obtain happiness for yourself.

Marital Distress:

I have been married for seven years. We have three small children together. The marriage has been rocky from the beginning. My husband has had infidelity issues since the beginning of the marriage. Throughout the years, we have been trying to build trust, but every so often I discover something that I'm not pleased with. Facebook messages, text messages, and his phone on silent when he's home. Not only is infidelity an issue, this man has a gambling problem.

We live in Houston and every weekend he travels to Louisiana to gamble. I feel like this is time away from the family, and he should spend that time at home. I'm trying to work with him and be a little more understanding, but I have reached my breaking point. He leaves for three or four days with little communication, and without even letting me know when he can't make it home that night. He feels that he is already on the road and doesn't need to contact me to let me know when he can't make it home. Now I'm feeling like he is back to his old tricks. I don't trust this man, and his disregard for my feelings has me feeling like its time to leave.

Question:

Can My Marriage Work Without Trust? Help!

Answer:

Trust is best defined as the belief that someone is reliable, good, honest and/or effective.

Trust is very important in any relationship and is an essential behavioral quality that is needed to make a marriage work. So, to answer your question, "Can Marriage Work Without Trust?"—my answer is no.

Unfortunately, you have entered and built a relationship based on mistrust and deception. You stated, "The marriage has been rocky from the beginning. My husband has had infidelity issues since the beginning of the marriage." I highlight your statements, not to judge you, but to emphasize my point. A relationship built on mistrust and deceit will be sustained based on mistrust and deceit. Trust is earned through action and unfortunately your husband's actions have not been trustworthy.

Healthy marriages prosper when two individuals make a commitment to protect the feelings and interests of each other.

Marriage is about being honest and thoughtful. A person who is willing to allow his or her partner to suffer is not trustworthy. Healthy marriages prosper when two individuals make a commitment to protect the feelings and interests of each other. Consideration and honesty should be non-negotiable in your relationship. Consideration demonstrates caring and honesty demonstrates transparency.

As you strive to cope with your marital discord, please remember that trust is essential to having a healthy and happy marriage. Also, please remember that actions speak louder than words. If you desire to make your life and/or marriage as prosperous as possible, you must learn to hold your husband accountable. Honesty is the best policy. Before you can demand honesty, you must be honest with yourself. I firmly believe that people treat you how you allow them to treat you. Being patient with your husband is noteworthy, however allowing him to be deceitful is not. Be mindful that pain and happiness are opposites. If what you want or desire causes you pain or makes you feel bad, then it cannot truly make you happy. Listen to your heart. If it hurts and you feel troubled that means that you are moving in the wrong direction.

Spend some time to figure out what you need and hold your ground. A confused and indecisive person will always be at high-risk for being abused. Learn to hold your ground and do not waiver in your position. If you do not stand firm, manipulative and selfish people will pick you apart. Do not trust in anyone who does not take your feelings and/or thoughts into consideration. The only way that trust can be restored in a marriage is if both individuals commit to a lifestyle of thoughtfulness, honesty and consideration. This behavior is easy for individuals who are selfless by nature. Selfish and self-centered individuals have to invest time in learning this behavior.

Marital Distress

I have been married to my husband for 12 years and he does not attempt to meet my emotional needs. Whenever I express my unhappiness with his lack of sensitivity and emotional coldness, he accuses me of being emotional and dramatic. When we first met, he was not very attentive to my emotional needs, but I brushed it off. Now, I am tired of brushing it off. I love my husband with all my heart, but I am not sure if we will make it if he does not show compassion and acknowledgement for my emotions. He rationalizes everything and I feel like we are on a battlefield. Can you please help me understand why he acts like this? Why do men struggle with being sensitive?

Question:

Why Do Men Struggle with Being Emotionally Sensitive?

Answer:

Unfortunately, you are experiencing what many women both single and married are experiencing, which is dealing with men who are emotionally challenged, but are psychologically skilled. You have probably noticed that some of the things that come out of your husband's mouth makes good sense from an intellectual standpoint, but, as you mentioned, lack emotional sensitivity. Men struggle with being sensitive because from the time we are little boys, we receive extensive psychological warfare training, but no emotional warfare training. Let me clarify what I mean.

The average little boy is instructed to "use his head to think" on an average of forty times a week. When little boys injure themselves, behave inappropriately or make bad decisions, they are quickly reminded of what they should have done differently. They are encouraged to *think*, but are rarely given any guidance about how they should *feel*. And unfortunately, this one-sided instructional process that focuses on nurturing the intellect continues as little boys transition into teens and men.

Some men hear the words, "Do you ever think?" an average of sixty times a week. After years of being instructed to think, little boys become men who have crafted the ability to successfully engage in psychological warfare. And before we present something to you, believe me, we have thought about it. We might not always come up with the best solution or sound intelligent, but we often think before we respond. The problem that most women have with men is centered on the fact that we often lack emotional sensitivity, not intellectual aptitude. Simply stated: learning how to identify and address emotions is challenging for most men because we operate in different reasoning spheres than you.

Men are often driven by intellect and believe that facts are equally important or more important than emotions. Objectivity or impartiality plays a vital role in how we act in our relationships. Men typically do not express sensitive or nurturing emotions without apprehension and pre-calculating the risk. Women, on the other hand, are often driven by emotions and believe that feelings are equally important or more important than facts. Subjectivity or emotionality play a vital role in the decision-making process of many women in relationships.

The difference in intellectual and emotional aptitude between women and men is what leads to all-out warfare. Men typically display very high intellectual aptitudes in relationships. In comparison, women typically display very high emotional aptitudes. Our desire to rationalize everything typically prevents us from feeling wholeheartedly and subjectively.

Through socialization, we have learned to rationalize inappropriate behavior, suppress our emotions and engage in tactical warfare in our relationships. We are groomed to be conquerors and unfortunately some of us take pride in being able to avoid and/or express sensitive emotions.

If you desire to save your marriage and further understand your husband, I highly recommend that you seek marital counseling. Your husband, like many other husbands, could benefit from receiving some sensitivity coaching. Please visit my website and contact me if you are interested in relationship coaching.

Marital Distress

I am speaking from the wife's point of view. My husband and I have a similar story to an earlier couple. Some details ring true—my husband had inappropriate text messages with a former neighbor and lied about it when I gave him the opportunity to discuss my suspicions. I have a very strong gut reaction that tells me when something is not right. Earlier in our marriage, he had an inappropriate conversation with a fellow church member at a party I did not attend, which resulted in her giving him on her phone number. That was the first time my gut instinct kicked in.

We have been married 12 years and have an 11-year-old son. I am no longer in love with my husband. He has been jealous and makes accusations that I am sneaky and untrustworthy. His words actually make me wish I were that girl looking to cheat and sneak around behind his back. This is not my M.O, I can't even remember what I had for breakfast this morning. I would be a lousy cheater.

I don't want a divorce, mostly for my son's sake. However, this marriage feels like a prison because he needs me to be someone I am not. He has had inappropriate interactions (texting and accepting phone numbers) with women I know and the jealousy is unbearable. It's insulting because I have been nothing but faithful to him, have raised his three daughters and am now raising his two grandsons and our son. And, I can't be trusted to have dinner with a girlfriend or a private conversation with our pastor?

What do you do when you have fallen out of love with your husband, but are not looking to break up your son's family unit?

Question:

Should I Stay in an Unhappy Marriage for the Sake of the Kids?

Answer:

It is important for you to spend some more time deciding what you want. You stated, "I don't want a divorce mostly for my son's sake. However, this marriage feels like a prison because my husband needs me to be someone I am not."

It is not uncommon for women to sacrifice their own happiness to make others happy, especially their spouses and children. While this selfless behavior is noteworthy, it can be very unhealthy for all that are involved. I say this to remind you that children are like sponges. They absorb our linkage both good and bad. If you are not happily married, know that your son is aware of and affected by your emotional disposition. Remaining married so that you do not break up your son's family unit might sound like the right thing to do, but do not minimize the potential negative consequences of exposing him to an unhealthy relationship.

You have to consider your son's present situation and future. Each child responds differently to divorce and/or being raised in an unhealthy family unit. No one can predict or accurately determine how your son will be affected by your decision to remain married or to leave. Given this, I strongly recommend that you consider what could be done to repair your marriage. Remind your husband that the both of you have an obligation to love each other, not only because it is the godly thing to do, but because your son's future prosperity in life-at-large might depend on it. Sometimes love can be restored by empathizing with the love in the hearts of our children. You and your husband brought your son into this world. This means that the two of you have responsibilities and obligations to him. Not just to remain married on his behalf, but to make your marriage as good as possible.

If you desire to save your family, please seek family counseling to help you repair your relationship. Before you throw in the towel, make sure that you have done everything within your power to rekindle your love. Deal with your problems head on and see what happens. If you cannot find happiness in your marriage, do not let your son deter you from doing what is best for you. Your personal happiness is just as important as your son's and husband's happiness.

The only way to fall back in love with your husband again is to explore the problems in your marriage and take responsibility for the role you may have played in creating your marital discord. Also, hold your husband accountable and demand that he work on his insecurity, trust and respect issues. If, after attending counseling, your emotional disposition does not improve, then move on knowing that you did what was in the best interest for all. I wish you the best and hope that you seek counseling. It can truly make a difference. I trust and believe in the benefits that one can receive from professional counseling because I have helped thousands of couples develop love again and indeed save what appeared to be unsalvageable marriages. Love is restorable for couples who cherish and nurture their relationships.

Marital Distress

My husband and I have been married for 14 years. I have no intention of leaving, but would like advice on how to overcome disappointments. When I married him, he had two children ages three and four. Within months of our marriage, his children came to live with us. While dating, I told my husband that I didn't like men with children because I want to be my husband's top priority. He says he didn't understand the extent to which I meant that.

Now some 14 plus years later, as his kids are preparing to leave for college, he still desires for me to love them but I can't—I really can't even like them. I have so much resentment for all the things that his kids have done to our lives and I see them as a burden, taking time and money away from our kids. I didn't have kids when we married, but we now have three together. His kids have always wanted their mother to be a presence in their life and constantly make excuses for her absence. This has always been hurtful for me as I have sacrificed so much for them, but they refer to her as "real momma." I know they are kids but, as I have explained to him, if a truck hits me and the driver is nine or 99, it still hurts the same. Is it possible for our relationship to flourish considering the strong resentments that I have and will seemingly never overcome?

Question:

Can My Marriage Flourish If I Am Filled with Resentment?

Answer:

Many of us go through life and love trying to figure out how to successfully overcome disappointment. In my work with couples, I have learned that one of the least effective methods for overcoming disappointment is to focus exclusively on one's own needs and to blame others for one's sorrow. We all were given the gift of *free will,* which allows each of us to make decisions free of others. You dated and eventually married your husband knowing that you desired to be with a man who did not have children. I do not point this out to chastise you or to judge you. I am simply reminding you that you freely entered into a situation that was not ideal for you. However, based on the fact that you have no intention of leaving your husband, you have allowed love to prevail. This is commendable, considering how easily people are walking away from their marriage these days.

Yes, it is possible for your relationship to flourish, if you are willing to put in the work to resolve your resentment. In my work with couples, I often remind them that disappointment does not destroy relationships; an individual's inability to cope with disappointment is what destroys relationships. As you journey toward another 14+ years of marriage, be mindful that romantic love is transitory, but true love is everlasting and requires ongoing work.

Listed below are a few coping strategies that might help you successfully overcome your disappointment and restore hope in your relationship:

1. Live in the Present and Focus on Your Future.
Yesterday is gone, today is now, and tomorrow is on its way. Therefore, you should use your time and energy wisely. Living in the present will enable you to enjoy the here-and-now and to stop obsessing over past events. Make the best of

your current situation and get fired up about your future because it is not tainted like your past. Remember that relationships are easy for people who cherish them, nurture them and live for them.

2. Explore and Understand Your Love Style. Knowing how you love will help you cope effectively, when faced with adversity in your relationship. Are you a *conditional lover* or an *unconditional lover*? Generally speaking, **conditional lovers** are impatient and will try to force or control relationship outcomes instead of allowing them to evolve naturally. Engaging in a relationship is viewed as a process to be controlled, not experienced. Conditional lovers plant the seed and then attempt to control how it grows. If conditional lovers are not capable of controlling outcomes, they turn their energy inwardly and focus on the self. This profound need to control outcomes often contributes to feelings of inadequacy, hopelessness, loneliness, helplessness, sadness, anger, greed, bitterness, fear and even hatred if efforts to gain control are unsuccessful. **Unconditional lovers,** on the other hand, are usually patient. They allow relationship outcomes to evolve naturally instead of trying to force or control them. Engaging in a relationship is viewed as a process to be experienced, not controlled. They plant the love seed and allow it to grow without attempting to control it. Unconditional lovers typically practice selflessness and use "we" talk: i.e., we want, we must have and we need. "We" talk is common among unconditional lovers. What is your love style?

3. Strive to Become an Empathetic Spouse. Empathy helps turn anger into sorrow. When interacting with your husband, try to put yourself in his shoes. Try to envision what life would be like from his perspective. Keep in mind that empathetic spouses treat their partners as assets. In contrast, non-empathetic spouses treat their partners as liabilities.

4. Learn to Forgive. Anger and resentment are negative emotions that enslave you. Forgive others and live freely. Letting go of anger and resentment is healthy for you and uplifts God's kingdom. Forgiveness is our Godly obligation. Also, forgiveness empowers you to take control over your emotions. As long as you harbor resentment, you are empowering those who hurt you. When you release resentment, you allow God's forgiveness to pour into your life. If you walk around holding grudges, you will deprive yourself of God's blessings. You must let go and move on. Remember that no one is perfect, including you. Each one of us has offended someone, so it is important to forgive others so God can forgive you. Pray for those who hurt you because they are also hurting themselves. When interacting with individuals who offend you or take you for granted, you should always strive to do right by them regardless of how they treat you. Life is not fair, but God is. You will be blessed.

As you strive to apply the strategies outlined above, remember that a stable mind is a prerequisite for a stable relationship. Drama begets drama and peace begets peace. It's easy to be problem-focused, but hard to be solution-focused. However, the latter is your saving grace and will save your relationship. If you desire to make your relationship as successful as possible, you must learn to live harmoniously with yourself and others in your household. Resilient women like you make life worth living for so many people. Know that you are the personification of optimism, the bearer of hardship and the healer of heartache. Thanks!

Marital Distress

I am married to a man that I've known for a good portion of my life and I love him dearly. We've only been married for a few months. However, things started out really crazy. I've already endured a cheating issue, but sought counseling. We decided to work through the cheating, despite my desire to walk. I've hung in thus far, but now this other issue is just eating away at me.

I'll explain. He was married to a woman for about seven years. They have a daughter together. He has visitation rights, pays child support and spends time with his daughter. The ex-wife does things that are just disturbing to me. For instance, it may not be his weekend to see the child, but the ex will request that he meet them somewhere, because the daughter wants to see him. I think she is the one who wants to see him and not the child. If it's not that, she'll request that he meet her to give her the child support money. It's always something.

Then, to top it off, she has no clue that he is married now and he will not tell her. He refuses to allow me to come with him to pick the child up for visits and he refuses to allow his ex and I to meet, even after I requested. He stated that they agreed to not bring others around when dealing with the child. I am his wife, not just some other person. It's just really crazy and hurtful to be honest. Am I being petty or is this really another issue?

Question:

My Husband's Ex Does Not Know We Are Married: Is This an Issue?

Answer:

No, you are not being petty, and yes, this is another issue! You are not feeling valued in your marriage because your husband does not respect you. One of the most important aspects of a healthy marriage is mutual respect. When respect is absent in a relationship, feelings of dismissal, rejection and bitterness surface. Once these feelings manifest, individuals either attack or become defensive. Obviously, this is problematic. Marriage works well when individuals feel respected and are functioning as teammates. Teammates work together to achieve a common goal. Each member of the team is respected for what he or she brings to the table. Life and relationship decisions are made jointly and each person feels valued. Teammate thinking is what makes marriage so appealing.

Your husband has a roommate mentality instead of a teammate mentality. Individuals with roommate mentalities believe that it is acceptable to function independently of each other because they see certain aspects of their lives as being separate. They take care of their kids. They manage their money. They put their best interests at hand first. This kind of thinking is counterproductive and will eventually destroy your marriage. Please be mindful that any relationship that lacks respect, dedication and teamwork will eventually end in pain and suffering.

You allow your husband to disrespect you by allowing him to keep you a secret from his ex-wife and from being a part of his child's life. As you stated, you are "his wife, not just some other person." Unfortunately, you continue to struggle in your marriage because your husband does not understand what it means to have a wife/teammate. There is no question that words communicate love, but so do actions. You need both to have a healthy marriage. First John 3:18 helps us understand this in the line, "let us not love with words or tongue, but with actions and in truth."

I highly recommend that you assertively demand respect from your husband and hold him accountable for his actions. Also, I encourage you to think about self-respect. If you do not respect yourself, you will probably struggle with getting respect from someone else. They say that insanity is doing the same thing over and over again and expecting different results. You cannot remain attached to an inconsiderate and disrespectful man and expect to feel valued. Please reflect on one of my favorite personal quotes:

Respect me or leave me because disrespect is not an option.

Remember that self-respect is the best kind of respect because you can show others what you desire and need. Establish a respectful relationship with yourself, and I assure you that you will feel whole and receive the respect that you desire. Please consider contacting me for coaching or visit my website and secure copies of **A Black Woman's Worth and Unconditional Love: What Every Woman and Man Desires in a Relationship.**

Marital Distress

I have been married 14 years. My husband recently cheated. We have been trying to work things out but I'm angry. He tried to find fault in me to justify his affair. He admitted that, only after I beat myself up over and over trying to find out what I did to cause it. A part of me wants to just divorce him! What should I do?

Question:

My Husband Cheated: Should I Divorce or Stay?

Answer:

It is understandable that you are angry and anyone in your shoes would feel the same. However, anger can and will debilitate emotionally, physically and spiritually if not dealt with effectively. In order to find peace and heal properly, please consider the following recommendations.

First, I recommend that you find healthy mechanisms to cope with your anger so that you can process clearly. Do whatever works for you, but consider the following: pray for peace, speak with family members or friends who are willing and capable of providing words of encouragement, or seek counseling.

Secondly, I recommend that you keep your head up and do not allow your husband to pass fault. I say this to remind you that cause-and-effect is not the same as influence and contribution. Every human being, including your husband, has *free will* and is capable of making decisions, free of others. Sometimes we do things that influence others' behavior, but we cannot control individuals; therefore, cause-and-effect does not apply to human behavior.

For example, some individuals claim that they cheat because they were denied sex or because they were not happy. While these factors might influence behavior, they do not cause individuals to cheat. This excuse-driven thinking is inaccurate because lack of sex or unhappiness do not *cause* cheating. Cheating occurs because individuals *choose* to cheat. The bottom line: your husband cheated because he wanted to. Think about what you can do differently to improve your marriage, but do not take on what you are not responsible for.

Third, I recommend that you develop a list of pros and cons for sustaining your marriage. I encourage this because we have a tendency to focus on the negative aspects of our relationship when we are hurting. Divorce might feel like the best option now, but by allowing yourself time to process the pros and cons of your marriage, you might find that it is worth saving.

Finally, I recommend that you do some research and invest in resources that can help you understand and gain insight into how to move forward. For example, if you have not already done so, I suggest that you secure a copy of **Still Standing (DVD)** by Lamar and Ronnie Tyler. The video is very encouraging and provides insight into how a diverse group of couples are STILL STANDING despite infidelity, chronic illness, financial crisis, blended families and more. I also suggest that you visit my website and secure a copy of my book, <u>Unconditional Love: What Every Woman and Man Desires in a Relationship.</u> From reading my book you will gain insight into what it means to receive and give unconditional love.

Some people argue that knowledge is power. I argue that the application of knowledge is power. Please equip yourself with power knowledge and apply what you learn. If you do these two things, I guarantee you that you will feel empowered. If none of the recommendations listed above help you heal, please do not hesitate to contact me for coaching.

Marital Distress

I have been married to my husband for two years; we have been together for eight. I recently found out that he cheated on me with two different women during the time we were dating. He swears he did not cheat while we have been married. I'm devastated by this situation. I feel like our whole relationship and marriage is a sham. I want to work this out though. We have a newborn, and before I found this out, we had never been happier. I'm not sure what to do, or how to feel. How do we work this out? What should I do? A few people have said that since he didn't cheat while we were married I shouldn't feel so bad. But I do. Any direction here would be great. I feel utterly lost.

Question:

I Discovered My Husband Cheated Before Marriage. What Should I Do?

Answer:

Cheating is one of the most difficult relationship challenges to cope with and recover from because it creates doubt and violates one of the most important core values that is needed to have a healthy relationship: trust. However, I encourage you to prevent past drama or distress from robbing you of a happy and blissful future. You said, "I want to work this out though. Before I found out, we had never been happier." With this in mind, I recommend that you focus on the positive aspects of your marriage because you cannot move forward while looking backwards. I am not suggesting that you ignore how you feel or minimize your husband's behavior. Feeling lost, devastated and confused are normal emotions considering what you are dealing with. The best thing that you can do to work this out and to heal properly is to give yourself time to process your emotions. Processing your emotions means that you should talk through them with your husband in a healthy manner, but avoid trying to make him feel guilty. Also, remember that feeling bad is okay as long as you do not act badly. Emotions drive behavior so it is important to learn to understand and share them in a positive manner.

Be careful of what you tell yourself and monitor your mental filter. Mental filtering occurs when an individual selects a single negative experience and dwells on it exclusively until his or her view of reality is clouded. Despite the fact that you have probably had some good times, you have decided to view your entire relationship negatively. For example, your husband cheated and you stated, "I feel like the whole relationship and marriage is a sham." This statement is negative and can contribute to negative behavior.

As you work through your challenge, remember that adversity builds resiliency, and resiliency is a precursor to success. Sometimes you will go through things in your relationship in order to mature and grow. This is your opportunity to grow. Develop a behavioral contract with your husband, agree to specific behavioral changes and reward each other for meeting specific goals.

It is easy to be problem-focused, but difficult to be solution-focused. However, the latter is your saving grace and will save your marriage.

If you have questions about your marriage, please send an email to me at **askdrbuckingham@gmail.com**

If you choose to send an email, please be mindful that my ideas, opinions or recommendations are not intended to be a substitute for seeking professional counseling or guidance. Any concerns or questions that you have about relationships or any other source of potential distress should be discussed with a professional in person. I am not liable or responsible for any personal or relational distress, loss or damage allegedly arising from any information or recommendations I make.

Appendices

Appendix 1

UNCONDITIONAL LOVE
MARRIAGE CREED

I _____ am responsible for making sure that my marriage lasts forever.

My expectations of my spouse will influence how I am treated.

It is my duty to love myself unconditionally and to do the same for my spouse.

I can and will become a change agent in my marriage, and give and receive the unconditional love that I desire.

I will make an effort to correct personal character flaws and accept constructive feedback in order to make my marriage last forever.

I realize that I am not perfect, but I deserve to be in a marriage filled with unconditional love!

Unconditional love starts with the self and is exemplified in marriage.

Appendix 2

Abusive Love Characteristics

As mentioned in chapter one, love does hurt, but not intentionally. To determine if you are in an abusive marriage, review the characteristics below. If any of the characteristics are present in your marriage, you should seek help immediately.

Types of Abuse

- Physical Abuse (inflicting physical discomfort, pain or injury): slapping, hitting, burning, punching, restraining, sexually assaulting, handling roughly, etc.

- Sexual Abuse (forced sexual contact, rape or incest)

- Psychological/Emotional Abuse (diminishing your identity and self-worth): threatening, insulting, name-calling, yelling, imitating, ignoring, isolating, etc.

Physical Abuse

- Pushes or shoves you

- Physically restrains you to prevent you from leaving

- Slaps or bites you

- Kicks, chokes, hits or punches you

- Locks you out of the house

- Abandons you in a dangerous place

- Refuses to help you when you are sick or injured

- Subjects you to reckless driving
- Forces you off the road or keeps you from driving
- Rapes you
- Threatens or hurts you with a weapon

Sexual Abuse

- Makes demeaning remarks about you
- Insists that you dress in a more sexually provocative way than you desire
- Calls you derogatory sexual names like "whore" or "freak"
- Forces you to strip when you do not want to
- Forces you to have unwanted sex with others or forces you to watch others
- Forces sex after beatings
- Forces sex for the purpose of hurting you with objects or weapons
- Commits sadistic sexual acts

Emotional Abuse

- Puts you down
- Makes you feel bad about yourself
- Calls you names
- Makes you think you are crazy
- Plays minds games with you
- Humiliates you
- Makes you feel guilty

Dominating Actions

- Treats you like a servant
- Makes all the big decisions
- Acts like the "master of the castle"
- Defines roles and responsibilities

Economic Abuse

- Prevents you from working
- Controls the money and makes you ask for it
- Gives you an allowance
- Takes your money
- Restricts your access to family funds

Uses Bullying and Intimidation

- Makes or carries out threats to do something to hurt you
- Threatens to leave you or to commit suicide if you leave
- Makes you drop charges
- Forces you to do illegal things
- Uses threatening looks or gestures to frighten you and control you behavior
- Smashes household items
- Abuses the children
- Displays weapons

Using Children

- Makes you feel guilty about your interaction with the children
- Uses the children to control your actions
- Threatens to take the children away from you

Using Isolation

- Controls what you do, who you see and talk to, what you read and where you go
- Limits your outside involvement
- Uses jealousy to justify actions

Minimizing, Denying, Blaming

- Makes light of the abuse and does not take your concerns about it seriously
- Denies abusing you
- Accuses you of the abuse

Manipulative attempts to keep you in the marriage or get you back if you leave

- Treats you very well; apologizes, does whatever you ask
- Treats the children well
- Seeks help – attends counseling

Personality Make-Up of Abused Victims

- Has low self-esteem

- Has traditionalist views
- Blames self for perpetrator's behavior
- Suffers from guilt, yet denies terror and anger
- Has severe stress reactions with psycho physiological complaints
- Uses sex as a way to establish intimacy
- Believes that no one will be able to help his or her resolve her predicament

Personality Make-up of Perpetrators

- Has low self-esteem
- Believes all the myths about battering marriage
- Is a traditionalist
- Blames others for his or her actions
- Is pathologically jealous
- Presents a dual personality
- Has severe stress reactions
- Uses sex as an act of aggression
- Does not believe violent behavior should have negative consequences

Reaction of Victims

- Denial
- Blaming self
- Ambivalence

Long-Term Effects of Abusive Marriage

- Physical
- Mental
- Economic
- Children

Appendix 3

Abuse Screening Questionnaire

If you answer yes to one or more of the questions below, please talk to someone you trust and seek help.

Has your significant other ever touched you without your consent?

Has your significant other ever made you do things you didn't want to do?

Has your significant other ever taken anything that was yours without asking?

Has your significant other ever scolded or threatened you?

Are you afraid of your significant other?

Do you have low self-esteem because your significant other belittles you?

Do you feel like you are emotionally unstable in your marriage?

Do you often feel depressed, anxious or angry due to relational conflict?

Do you feel hopelessness, guilt or sadness due to marriage stress?

Are you overly compliant or passive in your marriage?

Are you extremely aggressive or demanding in your marriage?

Are you extremely dependent on your significant other?

Seek help immediately if you are being abused.

Appendix 4

Defense Mechanisms

How do you protect yourself from emotional harm? By physical means or by using defense mechanisms?

If you are incapable of protecting yourself physically, you are likely to rely on defense mechanisms. Defense mechanisms are psychological strategies that manifest to help individuals maintain a "healthy" self-esteem or image of self. Individuals commonly use defense mechanisms to defend themselves from dreadful and anxiety-provoking thoughts, emotions and behaviors. Defense mechanisms are not necessarily bad unless they are counterproductive to your emotional or physical well-being. Most individuals use defense mechanisms when they are unable to cope with a particular situation. Listed below are some of the common defense mechanisms that my clients have used.

1. **Rationalization** – providing a logical or intellectual explanation as opposed to the real reason

    a. Ex. I am too busy to be in a marriage—when the real reason is that you are afraid

2. **Intellectualization** – avoidance of unacceptable or uncomfortable emotions by focusing on the intellectual aspects

    a. Ex. Focusing on the details of the divorce or separation—as opposed to the unhappiness and heartache caused by it.

3. **Projection** – placing unpleasant or unacceptable impulses within yourself onto others

    a. Ex. If you are losing an argument with your significant other, you state "You are stupid."

4. **Suppression** – pushing away uncomfortable feelings into the unconscious

    a. Ex. Trying to forget that your marriage is coming to an end or the pain associated with it

5. **Denial** – fighting against an anxiety-provoking stimuli by stating it does not exist

    a. Ex. Denying that your significant other's report that he or she does not love you anymore is correct

6. **Displacement** – taking out your impulses out on a less threatening target

    a. Ex. Talking to your significant other in a cruel manner because you are mad with or upset at your boss

7. **Repression** – placing memories into the unconscious

    a. Ex. Forgetting about physical, emotional or sexual abuse due to the trauma and anxiety

8. **Regression** – returning to a previous developmental stage

   a. Ex. Leaving the house and slamming doors; screaming and pouting when your significant other does not do as you wish

As mentioned, defense mechanisms are not necessarily bad—the way in which you express them determines if they will be counterproductive to you. It is important to be aware of defense mechanisms and learn effective coping skills to deal with the ones that cause distress and conflict in your marriage.

Scheduling For Seminars, Speaking Engagements or Film Screenings

Dr. Buckingham conducts seminars, speaking engagements and film screenings for groups, churches, and organizations throughout the year.

The **"Unconditional Love Marriage Seminar"** is one of the most requested seminars; however, Dr. Buckingham conducts seminars and speaks on a variety of topics related to marriage difficulty, personal growth, stress management, effective leadership and team building.

RHCS is dedicated to expanding the horizons of all humans!

To book Dr. Buckingham for your next event:

R.E.A.L. Horizons Consulting Service, LLC
P.O. Box 2665
Silver Spring, MD 20915

240-242-4087 Voice Mail
www.realhorizonsdlb.com

I hope this book has been a blessing to you and I welcome your comments.
dwayne@realhorizonsdlb.com

This book can also be purchased online at:

realhorizonsdlb.com

Amazon.com

BarnesandNoble.com

BooksaMillion.com

About the Author

Dwayne L. Buckingham, Ph.D., LCSW, BCD, is a psychotherapist and the Chief Executive Officer and Founder of R.E.A.L. Horizons Consulting Service, LLC in Silver Spring, Maryland. A commissioned officer in the United States Air Force, for nearly a decade he provided psychological assessments and treatment to over ten thousand individuals, couples, groups, and families worldwide. Dr. Buckingham currently serves as a commissioned officer in the United States Public Health Service and works at military medical treatment facility in Bethesda, Maryland. Dr. Buckingham is also an active member of the National Association of Social Workers and Kappa Alpha Psi Fraternity, Inc.

He is driven by the belief that every individual can improve his or her ability to cope with life challenges productively if given the opportunity and right support. Dr. Buckingham reminds individuals daily that a little understanding and education eliminates barriers and enables individuals to grow. Through coaching, consultation and training, he hopes to provide individuals with the knowledge and skills essential to establishing and maintaining a positive and productive lifestyle.

Dr. Buckingham conducts seminars for groups, families, organizations, and churches each year. Please visit his website at www.realhorizonsdlb.com for more information.

Made in the USA
Middletown, DE
23 September 2020